John Michael McDonald,
    September 1957.
from Bill & Helen.

SMALL MOMENTS

RICHARD CHURCH

has also written the following novels:

THE NIGHTINGALE
OLIVER'S DAUGHTER
HIGH SUMMER
THE PRODIGAL FATHER
APPLE OF CONCORD

THE PORCH
THE STRONGHOLD } A Trilogy, of which the first volume won the
THE ROOM WITHIN Femina-Vei Heureuse Prize

THE DANGEROUS YEARS

and for children:
A SQUIRREL CALLED RUFUS
THE CAVE
DOG TOBY

also the following history and critique of fiction:
THE GROWTH OF THE ENGLISH NOVEL

Other prose works include an autobiography:
OVER THE BRIDGE (Awarded the *Sunday Times* Prize for Literature)

and the topographical:
KENT
PORTRAIT OF CANTERBURY

Among his volumes of poetry are:
THE SOLITARY MAN
THE LAMP
THE INHERITORS (Awarded the Foyle Poetry Prize for 1957)

and he has edited such anthologies as:
POEMS OF OUR TIME
POEMS FOR SPEAKING

RICHARD CHURCH

Small Moments

Decorated with wood-engravings
by Joan Hassall

'There cannot be too much joy.'
Spinoza

HUTCHINSON OF LONDON

HUTCHINSON & CO. (*Publishers*) LTD
178-202 Great Portland Street, London, W.1

London Melbourne Sydney
Auckland Bombay Toronto
Johannesburg New York

★

First published 1957

*Set in eleven point Baskerville two point leaded
and printed in Great Britain by
William Brendon and Son Ltd
The Mayflower Press
(late of Plymouth)
Watford*

CONTENTS

SMALL MOMENTS

IN THESE DAYS of megalomania one is tempted to be ashamed to record the microscopic events, either private or public, which build up our human days as the cells of the coral multiply themselves into islands. It is said to be childish, egocentric, to stoop to such fragmentary evidence, neglecting the large events of politics and the economies and ideologies of nations. But even so, I suspect that we are all Gullivers in Lilliput-land, tied down, or drawn by tiny threads (made of character) towards our destiny, which in the accumulation become the destinies of States and Peoples. Thus I resist the temptation, and glory in my frequent preoccupation with unimportant matters, the sweet asides of life, the odd events and the fleeting moments.

What an un-aerated affair life would be without them. There would be no let-up from the text-book, the Government form, the massive orator. Let us escape together, dear reader and I, indulging our little-ness and learning in that adventure how rich, and rich again, are the moods of humility.

It was after the Christmas festivities had subsided, and the houseful of guests had gone, that I was reminded of these

1

contrasts. Do I not share with most people a feeling of *after-maths*, of slight psychic exhaustion, after a period of crowded pleasures and close neighbourliness? The enjoyment of them is intense; but then enjoyment is in itself a strenuous occupation, demanding every ounce of our energy, mental, physical, and emotional. To entertain our families and friends we have to give all that we have within ourselves, or almost all. And afterwards, we are like the widow's cruse, temporarily empty. It is then that the ever-repeated miracle takes place, the unaccountable refilling of the self within us. But we have to prepare for that miracle, and here again it is often not done deliberately, but by another act of external guidance, so that we wander away, in poverty of mood, to find ourselves seemingly but not actually by chance in the redeeming situation.

So I was led that night after Christmas. The last dinner-party was over, the last car load gone. The house was silent, dropped back into its own, personal domestic sounds, so familiar that we could no longer hear them. Before locking up, I went out into the lane, with my two companions, the Corgi and the white cat, to take a pace or two before creeping up to bed.

I felt the old year waning about me. That brings always a solemn condition of mind. Time looms up ominously, looms and passes, a great train in darkness, roaring and vanishing, taking part of us with it, our other, younger selves, so many selves that they have become strangers to us, except for an identity of regrets. As though to give body to this illusion, a desultory wind rose and fell, moaning in the telephone wires, rustling in the brittle holly tree, sighing in the bare hedges. Scarves of mist floated about the landscape, opal sleeves tinted by the moonlight. The moon herself was newly risen, or it seemed so when I compared her height with the great Dog Sirius who blazed above her.

His splendour so took my eye that I stopped walking,

stood in the middle of the lane, threw back my head, and stared at him. For a time, he was that star of which Wordsworth wrote in the lines:

'Fair as a star, when only one
Is shining in the sky.'

He stood alone because soft billows of cloud, sweeping across the heavens, had blotted out the rest of the constellations, and even the moon was veiled, like a queen in mourning. Her mood, however, touched the whole wind-moving sky, so that the clouds shone with a sort of ceremonial sorrow, sombre yet glowing, tossing up from time to time a slow-motion wilderness of gesture, so stately, so significant of something beyond my apprehension, that my heart rose to the tragic hints, and I felt once again the responses that I had thought to be vanished with youth; all those 'fallings from us, vanishings', by which the larger-than-us is brought home to our conscious selves.

But that was not the very moment, the small moment. No, it was to come and depart in an instant: but an instant of that eternity when the whole universe opens and we look as Dante looked in that last scene of the 'Divine Comedy', with the great music of the Revealed Paradise about him, seen as well as heard. In an English lane on a winter night, in the afterglow and depression following Christmas, there I stood with my cat and my dog, looking up at the night sky. Suddenly, with a wild break in formation, the swirling clouds opened, and there slid out from them the whole constellation of Orion, square and steady, with his belt glittering, his outriders like beacons, and following him, driving him on so briskly yet regally, his dog, the sun Sirius. There they hung, so clean-cut in the purple void, shining so fiercely that they seemed to dip and rise, dip and rise, by fractions of an inch, yet to ride steady, rushing westward through the vast silence. Then the clouds closed again, and the adventure was over. I had lived through an experience that might have taken a century to enact. I was enriched, humbled, my personal depression not dispersed but changed into something larger than myself, a quiet and utterly humble mood in which I resigned myself to the conquests by the years, the passing of all human achievements and possessions, and a recognition of the riches beyond them.

Then, half lost still, I felt a soft touch on my leg. The old cat, feeble with his age, was looking up at me, and the moonlight was spilled into his two great eyes. He murmured to me, and again lifted a padded foot to remind me where I was, and of my responsibility.

THE EMIGRANT

I AM JUST preparing to say good-bye to an emigrant. She is a very near and dear emigrant, who after graduating at her university in the old country of her birth, has decided that she needs wider spaces and more novel situations in order to exercise her ambition and personal faculties. The two people who had hitherto been responsible for her welfare have been inclined to look with a certain amount of vestigial misgiving at this proposal, just as father and mother thrush will sit on the home-bough and watch the initial flight of the fledgling. No amount of philosophy will quite dispose of this element of apprehension. It would be a curiously hard-feathered thrush who could burst into song at that precise moment.

There is always something of pathos about the emigrant. I recall Holman Hunt's (or is it Ford Madox Brown's?) famous picture of the family sitting on the steam-packet, under an umbrella, with the woman wrapped in a Victorian shawl, her eyes as large as saucers, and her hand clutching the shawl under her chin as though she were hanging to a life-line in desperation. Above her the man towers, and his eyes too are as large as dinner-plates under the dilation of grief. I could never bear to look at that picture without finding a lump in my

5

throat. Now I suspect that I could not look at all, at least until the farewells are over and some communication from the New World has been received to say that all is well, and wonderful, and that men and women there walk about robed in shining garments of compassion and friendliness.

And I think too of the hundreds of emigrant songs, in all European languages. They have the same refrain, the nostalgia, the desperate home-sickness, the fear of what lies beyond the hungry sea. But of course, that was long ago, when families broke up, and members were scattered as pioneers in unexplored lands west of the sunset, sailing in ships of oak, and trekking in waggons of oak, wind and horseflesh their only aid. Nowadays, we have no need for such feelings. How far, or rather how close, is Boston today to old England? I forget the mileage, and the *hourage*. But the contact is a mere bagatelle. I assure myself about that.

Safe in this assurance, I turn to the young emigrant, and suggest that for an hour or so she shall leave the cabin trunk, the suit-cases, the pressing-iron and the tissue paper, in order to come out for a last walk round the lanes, those arteries of her childhood, where she first looked upon the universe and found it to be a marvellously intricate concern, far bigger than she now thinks it to be. Her complaint was, lately, that it is such a small affair, this tiny island netted with roads, some of them two thousand years old. She has a craving for less sophisticated stretches of landscape, and I do not blame her, for at that age, when one is so confident in ones first achievement, the field of personal battle must needs be of vast dimensions in order to accommodate the grandeur, the amazing novelty of this new conflict with circumstance, out of which the newly accoladed warrior is to emerge triumphant.

The emigrant has shown a touching willingness to come for that last walk, and we have accordingly summoned the Corgi (who always suspects something which he will not find to his liking, for he has a morbid distrust of suit-cases, and all processes of packing) and we have ventured out into the autumnal woods.

Perhaps it is unfortunate that it should be autumnal; the last sight of the old cherry orchard, which is now flaming to its seasonal extinction; glorious, but unutterably melancholy. We turn from that, and walk together in silence down the lane past the green apple orchard, where the green survives, and the fruit, glowing like lanterns, is being picked by the farm-hands whose white ladders stand among the trees, like the scaling-rises in a fairy-battle scene by Uccello.

Below us, along the valley, a touch of mist is scarfed along the little stream, as it were an echo of the trickling water. It has an almost imperceptible movement, slow as time itself; slow as the years which have gone over the young head of our emigrant; and just as inevitable. I look beyond that ghostly reminder, and see the long stretch of the ancient forest, the King's Wood (the King being William Rufus of the eleventh century) whose massive oaks are still heavy under their chlorophyllic cloaks, now somewhat sombre after a summer of wear. Here and there a maple is set to mark the coming fall: a patch of ochre or crimson, like a spot of fire in a consumptive cheek. Along the hedgerow, too, I can see further reminders, urging me to accept the processes of nature, and the passage of the years, without wringing my heart in the agonies of farewell. The bryony berries, wandering along the hedges for many yards, are Dionysiac in their opulence. They are ready for twining in a maenad's hair, if a John Keats were here to do it. Blackberries hang in ebony clusters, each one touched with a glint of light from the afternoon sun, though that light is somewhat over-mature, somewhat lacking in certainty and definition. The cornfields are now fustian-covered stubble, waiting for the plough. That too, implies change, a relentless turning towards tomorrow's activity, tomorrow's hopes: but first, a long season of cold, and of fallow moods under the solicitude of winter skies. I must think of that too, and interpret the oracle offered me so gratuitously.

We do not say much to each other, my emigrant and I. A peculiar shyness seems to have overtaken us, as though after a lifetime, or at least *her* lifetime together, we are still strangers, and beginning an acquaintance, rather than ending it. But I am wrong there, we are not ending it. For the short passage now stretching between the Old World and the New, that used to be called The Steep Atlantick Stream, is not likely to interrupt a relationship that began with the cradle and has continued with such confidence that not even the impressive graduation at a university has been able to touch it with a suspicion of formality or a threat of change. No, these deep-rooted acquaintances, begun by mother nature, are not easily snapped off.

Our mutual shyness has some other cause than estrangement. Maybe it is due to a sudden revelation of understanding, of intimacy, now that we are about to part for the first time in the flesh. All, maybe, has been transferred to the spirit, and we are so rich together in our sharing of the past, our anticipation of the future, and our sympathy in the present, that no words, nor even a touch of hands, are needed.

A touch of hands! The phrase brings to my mind the bitter-sweet line of the poet:

'Whose hand is ever at his lips, bidding *adieu*.'

I think of the coming day, now so near, when the last good-byes have been whispered and the handkerchiefs are signalling more and more dimly as the ship leaves the quay. I am determined it shall be so; the hand at the lips, and not raised to cover the eyes that dare not look, knowing how vain it is to attempt to distinguish the emigrant among the passengers standing at the rail.

PEOPLE MUST GROW weary of reading about tourists' enthusiasms, for even in these days when letter-writing has been ousted by the postcard-habit, holiday-makers abroad are apt to try their hands once more at the rusty art, to ease themselves of the burden of rapture and wonder which accumulates from day to day among strange scenes and communities. The family at home has to wade through pages of geographical statistics, and cribs from the guide-books, with light relief in the matter of personal encounters and good meals.

But these temporarily uprooted folk are trying to get something through, to put on record experiences that are too big to be left unshared. Pleasure, like pain, makes us desperate, compelling us to break out in some form of creative gesture that snaps the fetters of habit. The results are invariably stilted and unskilled. I have been looking through some leather-bound albums of copperplate manuscript, diaries kept by the great-grandfather of a friend of mine, who with a companion set out in 1812 on horseback for a ride round the coast from his home at Eastbourne to Whitstable. Time has put a slight bloom on the flat surface of this traveller's prosy prose, and even his pencil sketches, some of them tinted with wash, are enjoyable in spite of their poor perspective, because of the figures wearing the clothes of the period. Even so, how dull it all is; and that was written in a time when letter-writing and diary-keeping was a practised art.

But, occasionally, something comes to life. A chance phrase or even one word does it; or maybe the greatness of the scene and moment. I think, for instance, of that passage in Goethe's autobiography where he describes his feelings when, after walking through the Alps, he comes at last to the

head of the pass on the southern side, and faces the Plain of
Lombardy. Italy lies before him. He attempts, 'after the
manner of dilettanti, to draw what could not be drawn, still
less make a picture, the nearest mountain-tops whose sides,
made visible by the melting snow, showed white furrows and
black ridges. Nevertheless, that fruitless effort has impressed
the picture indelibly on my memory'.

He does not try any verbal scene painting in his record of
that experience; but somehow the experience is passed on to
the reader, and I have found it remain in my memory too,
since I read the book thirty years ago. But that may be due to
the deeper significance of the moment. Here was this man of
genius, on the threshold of his mature life, with the astound-
ing variety and range of his interests, confronted with the *fact*
of Italy, the land about which he had learned so much during
his eighteenth-century boyhood and youth in Germany. For
in those days the only culture that was at all valued in
Germany was the culture of Italy; its music, its art, its
history, and its unbroken link with the 'grandeur that was
Rome'.

Nobody of any imagination or sensibility can fail to share
that experience with the young Goethe. It is based on anticipation. We have seen the backgrounds to the pictures
painted during five hundred years by the masters of Tuscany,
Venice, Rome. We have read in the literatures of Europe
again and again of the Italian scene, its towns and peoples.
The fantasy of preconception built up by this is something so
solid that a sort of second self is established, a self as real as
that which peeped out one day when young Coleridge was
caught moving down the Strand with his arms making fish-
like movements. When asked what he was doing, he said
breathlessly, 'I am swimming the Hellespont.'

That is how we first enter Italy, and the problem is always,
how shall we introduce the two to each other, the real Italy of
soil, air, people, and the Italy set even more solidly in our

imaginations, deep-rooted in the dawn of our consciousness?
I am still in process of making that introduction; and the
task is not easier because the likeness between the two is so
often confusing, uncanny. When preconceptions turn out to
be like the reality, the result is something that startles us, by
opening prospects of still more revealing unities. A recognition where none is expected can be terrifying.

The outstanding recognition on going to Italy is, of course,
that this land of peasants and medieval towns and villages is
truly the foundry of European civilization, not only in the
obvious, visible things such as cathedrals, palaces and gardens,
but in matters of domestic and social detail; goods and
chattels, manners and devices. In a thousand ways we see
things that are immediately familiar, and we know at once
that so much of what we had accepted in our home country
as native, is after all only a semi-barbarous imitation 'of the
Roman custom', an imitation set perhaps two thousand years
ago when Europe *was* the Roman Empire, except for the
gothic darkness north and east of the Alps.

But the two Italys, that of the inward and that of the outward eye, by their play each upon the other, create in our
minds a fourth-dimensional world of beauty and symbolism
which is almost too much to bear. The impact of the two, as
they half-fuse into one while leaving a stereoscopic, blurred
margin, is like that of the greatest music and poetry, or any
other experience which happens to be more than we can take.
It is that impact which I am trying to record here, for if it can
be pinned down, then something has been done toward the
definition of a whole European value, that entity for which
the Council in Strasbourg is establishing a machinery of
preservation, that *Idea* whose survival has been determined
upon because it holds the seed of human civilization, so far as
it has grown in the western world.

To begin with, this coming out of the north into the south
is in itself an awakening to a larger way of life. It creates a

sixth sense, and adds another dimension to memory. C. E.
Montague defines this elementary stage of the experience of
going to Italy. 'Perhaps,' he says, 'to lie awake, as the old
do, through English August dawns, remembering many past
awakenings in trains when day was breaking over Delamont
or Porrentruy, and houses half seen through the blanching
windows seemed to have taken wide eaves upon themselves
during the night; brooks, silent all across France, had begun
to make little jovial noises, and clouds had come down from
the sky to tumble about on the fields. To live with dim ghosts
—quite kindly ghosts, but dim—of the warm-blooded hours
of old autumn journeys to Italy, up to meet the bleaching
chill that creeps in October from Goeschenen down to
Lucerne; and then the plunge into the tunnel's murmurous
darkness under the very hub, the middle boss of Europe, the
rocky knot in which all her stone sinews are tied at their ends
into one central bunch; and then the emergence, translating
you out of a Teuton into a Latin world, from grizzled wintry
tonelessness to burnished lustre, all the lingering opulence of
sun-fed brown and yellow, purple and crimson and rose—
Airolo, Bellinzola, Lugano, all aglow and deep-hearted, like
rubies or wine, in that Giorgionian champaign of olive and
mulberry.'

That passage catches something of the physical transla-
tion, for Italy is indeed a land of 'burnished lustre', though
not necessarily more colourful than the north, nor even more
beautiful. I cannot say what the difference is. A Kentish
chequer of fields and hedgerows, with its soft intimacies
blended by the moist air, has something far more poetic and
elusive than Italy can offer. But the lustre, the quality of
flowing life, of blood in the veins, hot and dangerous, which
lies even in a bare stretch of hills and sun-bleached plain
south of the Alps, comes upon one with a sort of *anterior*
recognition. It is as though we knew this earlier than we
knew our birthplace in the north, and that therefore it is

more associative with our humanity, both past and present, because it has a racial authority.

The depth, the mystery of it, is the theme of the opening paragraph of Frazer's *The Golden Bough*, that enormous work which sets out to find the source of all religious symbolism. Frazer pictures 'the scene, suffused with the golden glow of imagination in which the divine mind of Turner steeped and transfigured even the fairest natural landscape, is a dream-like vision of the little wood-land lake of Nemi—"Diana's Mirror"—as it was called by the ancients. No one who has seen that calm water, lapped in a green hollow of the Alban Hills, can ever forget it. The two characteristic Italian villages which slumber on its banks, and the equally Italian palace whose terraced gardens descend steeply to the Lake, hardly break the stillness and even the solitariness of the scene. Diana herself might still linger by this lonely shore, still haunt these woodlands wild.'

From that touch of atmospheric incantation, the anthropologist proceeds to a line of argument and illustration that is to occupy the whole of his long life, during a search for the fundamentals of the relationship between man and nature. In the course of that process, everything that has been given the identity of magic, a secondary but more important recognition than that of the physical, is examined. And we see that most of these symbols, of tree, stone, air and water, are the elements that make up the Italian landscape, the Italian people and way of life.

A passage from one of Shelley's letters illustrates what I mean. He is describing a scene near Naples, the Caccia d'Ischieri, to his friend Thomas Love Peacock. 'It is a royal chace, surrounded by steep and lofty hills, and only accessible through a wide gate of massy oaks, from the vestibule of which the spectacle of precipitous hills, hemming in a narrow and circular vale, is suddenly disclosed. The hills are covered with thick woods of ilex, myrtle, and laurustinus; the polished leaves of the ilex, as they wave in their multitudes under the partial blasts which rush through the chasms of the vale, glitter above the dark masses of foliage below, like white foam of waves upon a deep blue sea. The plain so surrounded is at most three miles in circumference. It is partly occupied by a lake, with bold shores wooded by evergreens, and interrupted by a sylvan promontory of the wild forest, whose mossy boughs overhang its expanse, of a silent and purple darkness, like an Italian midnight; and partly by the forest itself, of all gigantic trees, but the oak especially, whose jagged boughs, now leafless, are hoary with thick lichens, and loaded with the massy and deep foliage of the ivy.'

There again the epithets denote an attempt to capture the secret of that sullen, brooding boldness of the Mediterranean landscape, a characteristic present in all the variety of scene round the 'wine-dark sea'. Giorgione's pictures, the first easel pictures, are rich with it, and so too are the backgrounds to Tintoretto's dramatic and crowded canvases.

This is the world which opens to us when we come to the Gateway of any of the mountain passes across the Alps, and look south toward Rome. Rome; the very sound of that mighty name gives the dominant of the symphony. For that is what one may call Italy, a symphony of civilization, a unit comprising all that Western Man has done, and dreamed of doing, under the compulsion of nature, and that force even more powerful than nature, the sun-maddened power of our human imagination as it seizes the fire, and defies the gods even while it worships them.

Unless we are utter barbarians, we all look that way, and take that path to Rome, where the wolf first suckled the founders of Europe and our golden traditions of life, art and philosophy. The barbarism is again approaching that centre, not only politically, but in every way, through the hearts and minds of a generation shaken by the world wars, and ignorant of the symbols which have been the script of European civilization for nearly three thousand years, since Homer began the record. We who know the values, and where to find them, need to be vigilant in the coming dangerous years.

WITH WHAT EAGERNESS we went away for a month's holiday. After a wet winter, and a coincidence of professional and family anxieties, we suddenly decided to escape for a while, thus to look at our affairs, and the weather over our personal sky, from the outside. The packing of bags began with the usual excitement and discussion. 'Do you *really* need that unmanageable hat-box?' And the *riposte*, 'Is it necessary to lug around quite that number of books?' All part of the mutual thrill; as it were a flapping of wings preparatory to flight.

And then the drive to Dover on a misty, moisty morning through the lanes of homeland, followed by the Channel crossing with the sea kind and participant in the holiday mood. After that, the familiar smell of French tobacco on the quay at Calais, and the first meal on a French train after our bags were safely stored in our sleeper which should be our camp for the next twenty-four hours. Then the journey through beloved France where spring was still tardy. Rows of poplars touched with finger-tip pink buds; marshy tracts flesh-tinted with the cuckoo-flower; farms within their own courtyards, half medieval fortress and half squalid slum, but wholly beautiful; villages near and far, in the plain or perched on hillsides, with their ancient churches and domains each with a *manoir* seemingly built of ivory; peasants fishing and ploughing; all these ancient and recognizable features of a mighty nation flashing past the windows of the carriage until darkness came down and we crept into our bunks, to listen through the night to rhythms, bumps, vague cries at vaguer stations, with an occasional shrill lamentation from the locomotive that made sleep impossible even had we

16

desired it. And we only half-desired it, for to sleep would have been to lose something of the adventure that comes afresh every holiday.

And, as always before, time began to play its tricks. No sooner were we set out from our own door than time raced like the wheels of an old clock from which the pendulum has been removed. Routine is the pendulum, I suppose, which makes our home-life and working-day so steady, so slow and regular. There we were, no sooner started than arrived, nearly two days later, in Florence. And within an ace of reaching there, we discovered we had been there for three days yet might have been there for three months, so familiar were we with several streets and buildings, and a favourite restaurant. This complication of Chronus was further tangled by excursions to other places, Assisi, Perugia, Pisa, and outlying spots where friends invited us to admire their hillside gardens, retreats such as Virgil and Horace must had enjoyed two thousand years ago. Some of the gardens looked that age, especially one, at Bellosguardo, overlooking Florence, though I know that it was a mere three centuries old. I shall never forget those terraces and stone balustrades, stained with moss and brushed by fronds of cypress; great Roman vases filled with azaleas and camelias, wisteria dropping down like falls of amethyst from terrace to terrace, giving on to bosquets and groves where statues glimmered in the shade and trees shaped like gigantic green candle-flames stood without flickering against the sky. And beyond all this, stretched below in a lake of dazzling sunlight, lay Florence like an intricate cameo on the bosom of the hills, a city of topaz, emerald and gold.

Days began to form into a traffic block, racing up, halting, and piling their experiences upon us until our minds were buried in the confusion of events and riches. When did we do this; when see that? Whom did we meet today? No, that was last Monday! So it went on. And alas, the holiday went on too, a feast of encounters, scenes, contacts with grandeur and beauty that cannot be described because in our modern world we lack the unself-consciousness to do it. Who were these Renaissance citizens with their glittering princes, we asked each other, that amid anarchy, political corruption and a total lack of hygiene, could stamp the face of Tuscany and Umbria with the seal of splendour and a pride that even today, with that seal cracked and no more than a museum relic, forces the tourist into a mood of reverent wonder? We sought the answer, and did not find it. Time would not permit. Time would not permit many other inquiries and exaltations to work out their consummation. There we were, wandering about like children in Aladdin's cave, staring up at vast halls, frescoes, carvings, appalled by the richness, the expertize, the genius and craftsmanship that adorned five centuries of a civilization that can never be imitated and will never be surpassed.

All that in a holiday, a month in which the problems of self and our local dilemmas were cancelled out by this superb draught of impressions. It was a throwing open of windows in a room where the confinements of winter had coagulated. The great winds of the life and art of a vanished people came roaring through our timid casements and swept our cares away. How happy we were, among the courteous Tuscan people, who have a faculty for entertaining visitors. We stared at the handsome materials in the shop windows (long unfamiliar to English eyes), we enjoyed the inspired cooking of good food, we let the skill and beauty of the Tuscan way of life penetrate the pores of our minds as it were by a kind of osmotic pressure, as the sun comes down upon starved fields, or a drop of rose-attar works its aromatic way through a wardrobe of tired garments.

And then time played its last trick. Before we realized what was happening, we were in a sleeper once more, rushing north through the day and night, but without the sense of adventure. The Channel crossing this time was less friendly. A north-easterly wind blew; the sea was made of cold but molten lead that heaved and heaved again, so that we arrived at Dover wondering if . . . if. . . . But no, we were not capable of wonder. It was a matter of staggering to the car, faintly recognizing something of ones own, and subsiding into it, grateful for a promise of home.

That was it. At that moment we realized what is, after all, the most intimate and penetrating experience during the whole of a long holiday. It is the realization that one is home again; and it comes just before the very last moment when, the final second of time ticking out before the return to the normal sequence of the hours and weeks and months, we touch the threshold and know that we are back, and the holiday finished.

The drive home after that, through the Kentish lanes where spring still was delayed, became a mood of reminiscence gradually giving place to an eagerness far more compelling than that with which we had started out a month before. As we drew near, and nearer, noticing a tree here that was familiar, there a cottage whose owner was an old acquaintance, then finally almost the very clods of earth in the fields, we knew that here was the crown of our pleasure, after all the junketings and ecstasies; thus to be back in a quiet place, among our own things, small enough and humble enough after the splendours of Renaissance Italy and the flowers of the Mediterranean culture. Small, but our own, and no longer saturated with care.

HELPING A TREE

TEN YEARS AGO, when bringing a sloping meadow partly
into my hillside garden, I planted a new turf walk with a
border of lilac trees; double purple and double white, so that
in Maytime we could take a stroll amid a blaze of banners
under perfumed air. Ten years gives young trees ample time
to take a firm hold upon life, and to exert their personalities
in relation to their environment. All but one of my lilacs
have done so. That one, the last in the row, nearest to the
sun as he moves through the valley every day, is a poor thing.
It began like the others, and for two or three years put out its
great confections of dazzling white bloom, and threw up
healthy suckers during the later months of the growing season.
But on the fourth year it began to show signs of distress.
Round its bole it exhibited pale blotches. Its blossoms
diminished, until they resembled farthing dips rather than
blazing candelabra. Promised leaf and new wood failed to
develop. Now, in the eleventh year, this tree is a stunted

creature, so lackadaisical that I fear it will not survive another summer. It is budding, of course, but those tell-tale blotches round the bole, and patches of fungi farther up the trunk, are sufficient warning that something must be done if this poor creature is to maintain its place in the rank of flower bearers.

I have been making that attempt at succour. What a satisfying occupation it is. Knowing that I risked losing the tree; for it was already showing lips of green at the tip of each bud; I decided nevertheless to deal with it thoroughly. At first I intended merely to loosen the soil round its roots and drain them with an addition of builder's rubble. But on ex-amination of the top roots I found such a state of decay that without further hesitation I dug deeply round the tree, summoned muscular help, and lifted it bodily out. Half the roots were rotted.

I then dug deep into the subsoil, looking for wire-worm and leather-jacket, those two subtle enemies of all roots. The soil was not so infested, nor was it waterlogged as I had sus-pected it might be. I tipped in first a barrow-load of broken brick and mortar. Then I mixed a load of sand, lime, peat and bone meal, and replanted the lilac tree in this light setting. There it stands today, after the upheaval, looking already somewhat happier, almost grateful. I have broken all the regulations about not moving plants that are showing signs of rising sap. But I am convinced that my depressed little lilac will not suffer by my intrepidity. I am prepared to avow it on my green thumb.

Afterthoughts about this operation in the garden remind me, if I need reminding, what a life-giving activity is this work out of doors among the flowers and vegetables. To one who is condemned (happily enough) to a sedentary occupation for most of the working day, with little tangible result to show for the habitual effort week after week, year after year, the relief of turning to another activity such as the garden offers is in-describable. It is such a common solace, too, that to attempt to discuss it is trite. Who doesn't know of its benefits? But these universal pleasures and benefits are so apt to be taken for granted that we forget to mention them, and in the end we accept them without even the consciousness of gratitude. To be grateful is to be offering thanks; and that in itself is a form of prayer, bringing additional joy thereby. To appreciate any gift is to double that gift; more indeed, for the physical fact is promoted to infinity.

So it is when I go out to my garden, particularly after some experience that has made a drain on my mental and nervous resources. There may have been an occasion causing strain; doubts, suspicions, anxieties, such as no man or woman can escape, nor should wish finally to escape, may have been suddenly loaded upon me like the burden upon the back of travelling Christian on his way towards the Shining City. No matter! I go out after the crisis, or even before it, if I want to gather strength; and I turn to the needs of these flowers and trees which I have brought together as a choral body of living beings, each with an offering of colour, perfume, fruitfulness and shade. Since they are living, they are incalculable. Two and two in a garden do not make four. The arithmetic of the magical soil of our good earth is different from that. Our human progressions, cemented by logic, have their rigid advantage, no doubt. But it is the very element of doubt in the nature of the soil and all that springs from it, which brings the joy, the rapture, the unexpected moment full of worship and thanksgiving. I am reminded by its processes of the miracle of the loaves and the fishes.

And even when there come these chagrins, these experiences such as I have had with my desultory lilac tree, the effect is not a mere mechanical one of drab assurance. I had hopes, for example, that this end member of the gay border of Schubertian blossom would be the most sturdy of the lot. But the disappointment did not deter me. These plants are like people; we are never quite sure of their reaction. And in that rich uncertainty lies the secret of our contact with them. It is made fertile, expectant, exciting. How strange, perhaps even dreadful, it would be to live with a person whom we had been able to circumnavigate completely! It would be like living with a right-angled triangle! Or at the most a conic section. But a human being, and a lilac tree, are acquaintances and contacts about which we can never say 'I know that. I have mastered it, read it, resolved it. I know the answer.'

We do not know the answer when the problem involves a living creature. And it is my belief that we should be as thankful for this as for anything life offers or withholds from us. In the uncertainty lies the whole of our faith, our apprehension of something outside the field of logic, of determinism. We accept this acquaintance, this relationship, this responsibility, and we accept it with a sort of inspired ignorance; aware that we do not know, and strong in that lack. It is not easy to make clear to our fellow-creatures how powerful that acceptance-in-faith can be. There may be no way of expressing it through the intellect and the ceremony of speech. That is why I am so happy in the action of going out to the garden, where I can demonstrate for my own satisfaction, merely by dealing with a failing lilac tree, that my faith is infinite, and that with these two hands clasped around the spade, I am returning my thanks for the certainty that lies in the heart of all uncertainty.

CRAB-APPLE BLOSSOM

THERE WAS NO doubting the fact that when I returned to England from my travels, I found cause for gloom. I had come home expecting so much. While wandering about the superb towns of Tuscany and Umbria, those cameos carved by Renaissance artists from material dropped so lavishly by the Romans and Etruscans, I soon discovered that excess of riches, both in natural scenery and the works of human genius, can begin to work upon ones nerves like any other excess, to produce a kind of lethargy, a callousness. I sighed for barren spaces and empty rooms. But being human, I went on with my gluttonous explorations into art galleries, arrogant palaces, gardens aching with the song of the nightingale, and the foothills of the Apennines dusted with snow showers.

Spring was late even so far south, and it was not possible to sit in comfort outside the cafés, to rest weary feet after each peregrination round marble-floored *salons*, with neck craned and back bent, gazing at ceilings as crowded with figures as Chaucer's *Canterbury Tales*. I recall two days spent in Perugia, sitting in the hotel while the rain drummed steadily down. From time to time, impatient of this waste of precious moments, I crept out under the shelter of massive walls,

to visit the cathedral, or the Town Hall, to study the paintings
of Perugino, that most famous son of this mountain city. But
it was a damp, almost a squalid adventure, and it served only
to increase my impression that Perugia is a strange, arrogant,
and grim survival from the most sinister side of the Roman
Empire. At the bottom of the town stands an Etruscan Gate.
It is a relic of some *civitas* even older than the Roman. And it
looks it. The arch rises up for some fifty feet, blocks of dry-set
masonry held together by their own weight, each one a
wedge weighing many tons, so that the pressure of the
centuries consolidates this gloomy gateway.

Above the arch loom great bosses of stone, the only
decoration until at a vast height above them, the masonry
breaks into an open colonnade, behind which a balcony
gives on to some human windows; but of a humanity long
since departed. How many thousands of tons this fortress-
portal weighs, I cannot imagine: but the roads converge to
that arch, dipping as though sagging under the pressure.
Through the gateway the aspect is that of a tunnel, for the
walls of the town must be at least twelve feet thick, and
beyond that other walls face each other for many yards up
the narrow lane that runs to the height and centre of the city.
I almost looked up, expecting to read the words that Dante
read over the portals of Hades, 'Abandon hope, all ye who
enter here.'

To come upon that sight in weather which blanketed the
hills with a sultry fog of mist and rain, was to feel the utmost
enmity of both nature and man. I was haunted for days
after, and I doubt if I shall ever be able to think of Perugia, or
even to visit it again, without recalling that first aspect of its
massive antagonism to the stranger seeking to enter.

Nor did the mood lift when I returned to Florence, the
City of Flowers, for the rain persisted, and the cold came
down from the Apennines. I found the River Arno moaning
over its several weirs through the town, its grey waters

C

reflecting a leaden sky. The walls of the ancient Palazzo of the Signoria gleamed in the wet, giving it the aspect of a prehistoric monster of predatory mood.

Coming north to Paris, I was pursued by this malignance, for there the Place de la Concorde was a dreary waste of wind-swept pavements sodden with rain, marked by the usual fountains, but now they were moulting in discouragement. The trees along the Champs-Élysées dripped, every young leaf pointed with moisture like a rheumy nose. The Gay City? I took train and was carried to Calais, and as we skirted the sand dunes between that port and Boulogne, I craned my neck trying to diagnose the condition of the English Channel, that notoriously fickle stretch of water which is faithful only in one matter—that it keeps invaders away from our island shores, or at least has done so for the past nine hundred years. I saw little, because the fog and rain were still being snorted from out of that savage mouth of the Etruscan Gate of Perugia—due north to the shores from which I now pro-posed to escape. Escape I did; but at a price. I found the Channel a mass of cold but liquid steel, awkward and sullen, heaving itself about sulkily, here and there, front and side, top and bottom. There was no meaning to it. And no sign of the farther shore! Only mist, rain, and chaotic upheaval! That crossing is alleged to take an hour and ten minutes. I can only say that such a statement proves the total inadequacy of statistics.

However, I reached Dover. I know it was Dover because I looked up, and saw looming out of the storm a pallid front, the walls of Shakespeare Cliff, where once King Lear looked down in his madness, and saw the samphire gatherers at their 'dreadful trade'. I almost saw them too. I was in a condition to see anything.

Having tottered through the Customs, and succumbed to several porters, I found my car waiting outside the station, veiled in a net of raindrops. This was a foretaste of home, and

I found myself again. From that moment something began to hint at changes in the mood of the universe. I heard an English thrush fluting cheerfully as the car climbed out of the port and sped along the cliff tops towards Folkestone. Leaving Folkestone, it turned inland, and I began to recognize the scenery with an intimacy which I had not felt for a month. Here again were the by-lanes, winding unsoberly about and about, edging odd fields and copses, doubling round cottages and farms.

And at this stage the rain stopped. At first I did not notice it, for the wind-screen still streamed and the road ahead lay shrouded in mist. But as we moved inland, the air cleared a little, and at last we could see signs of differentiation between earth and sky. Then colour came back into the world. English hedgerows ribboned past us, pale green still, belated in their foliage, March-like in May. The mists shredded out, thinned and disappeared. The clouds withdrew and formed into familiar shapes, billow upon billow, above the welkin. The sullen and forbidding tunnel of the Etruscan Gate no longer seemed to be breathing dragon's breath northward over Europe. Instead, as we approached still nearer the fields of home, a gleam of timid sunlight broke out of the heavens, small as a dove coming down. It alighted in front of us, and we saw it settle on a crab-apple tree standing waiting in a still leafless wood. And that tree was mantled in blossom, delicate pink and white, like a girl-bride. I knew then that Perugia lay far away, and I no longer shivered at the thought of the Etruscan Gate.

A FRIEND FROM France, while on a visit last summer, asked me to introduce him to some 'of the English peasants'. It was one of the few points on which, as a scrupulous host, I failed him. I could not show him an English peasant because there are none. It is hardly an historical exaggeration to say that there never have been any. Even when the Feudal System, brought over by William of Normandy in the eleventh century, was laid over the Saxon community system, it failed to make our island society conform completely to that of the mainland of Europe. That little strip of water which the French call *The Sleeve* has had a great influence in the making up of our national character. It has acted as a kind of filter, holding back some strains, permitting others, with the result that every wave of invading forces has left a residue that is subtly different from its original on the Continent. The Normans came, but their land-grabbing barony had to settle into a different kind of relationship with the field-folk, from that between master and man abroad. Life in the great medieval religious communities, so much of it close to the soil, took on a special quality and habit in England. When the Flemish weavers were invited here by Edward III in the fourteenth century, they accommodated themselves in such a way to the national life that they too became unique. In all these mixings the resultant flavour was a special one, like nothing else in the European comity. It was English. I do not know how else to describe it.

I have just come across a book, however, which helps toward a definition. It is called *A Yeoman of Kent* and is written by a native of Kent. He is rightly to be called a Kentish Man, to distinguish him from a Man of Kent. The demarcation is important to anthropologists and to local patriotism. A Kentish man is born in that part of Kent lying west of the tiny, tributary river the Medway, which flows into the Thames at Sheerness, near the Naval Dockyard. Folk born east of the Medway are Men of Kent, said to be of a darker countenance, owing to their Jutish blood. There is comparatively little friction between the two peoples; no customs barriers, no iron curtains. I have friends on both sides of the stream, and our intercourse is untrammelled.

I have determined, when opportunity permits, to make myself known to this Kentish Man, Mr Ralph Arnold, in order to discuss with him this absorbing question of the nature of the English countryman who is neither a peasant nor a serf. We call him a yeoman, and glib people will say that he is different from the Continental rural worker only because he is somewhat better off, owing to the historical fact that his ancestors, by commuting the personal service demanded by the Feudal System, and in its place paying a money rent so that they knew where they were and were able to set about getting a little something at the back of them, thus set him on the road to freedom.

But that is not enough. The core of the problem remains. I want to ask my neighbour Arnold if he agrees with me that this yeoman spirit (and *not* the mere economic) contains the germ of that *something* (still undefined) which is the seed of the English-speaking people throughout the world; something which took root in New England and sprouted and flowered in a particular way so that it is recognized as of the same stock whose principal characteristic is a marked indifference to theory, and a steady belief in good works, whether it be on the land, in the city, or in the seat of Government.

But I know that is a question which would occupy us indefinitely; leading, no doubt, to comings and goings north and south (for he lives, I discover, in the village about which he writes in his book) in the course of which we shall both increase our knowledge of the geography, ornithology, history, agriculture and every other aspect of the life of our beloved county (some still call it the little *Kingdom* of Kent).

The village about which he writes is Cobham, famous for the magnificent palace of Cobham Hall, seat of the Earls of Darnley (everybody knows what part that family has played in the royal story of Scotland and England). The present Earl Darnley no longer has thirty servants indoors and an army of retainers on his farms and park. He keeps up a busy life, however, as farmer, nurseryman, and horticultural specialist. He combines this with the traditional hospitality of the great houses of England, as I know to my pleasure, for once, when I was collecting material for a history of the county which I was commissioned to write, I called casually at Cobham Hall, after wandering about among the millennial oaks in the park, and was shown round the house by its owner, who gave up an afternoon to the purpose. Even in that time I was not able to savour fully of the architectural riches; but I came away drunken upon the vision of Inigo Jones and William Kent at their best.

Mr Arnold, however, has concerned himself not with the aristocratic aspect of English rural life. He has concentrated on a middle course, choosing not the palace, nor the cottage, but a yeoman's house in the village. This house is called Owlett's, and it was built in 1492 by a family of Protestant faith who migrated from France about that time. Their name was Owlett, and they were silk weavers, prosperous folk who objected to fanatical interruption of their craftwork by the religious disturbances in their native land. Since reading Mr Arnold's book, and commenting on it in the press, I have had a letter from a member of this ancient family (he still bears the name), an incident which shows how continuity is still a factor in our national life, in spite of the upheavals abroad (and so near!) during the twentieth century. To the English yeoman, a few hundred years are a matter of tree-growth, nothing more.

Now I could write on at length about the tale of this house, how it passed from the Owletts to the Hayes at the beginning of the eighteenth century, and what these purely farming, and therefore yeoman folk, did during their occupation of the house until it passed from them to the Bakers, the last of whom, a famous architect to whom I have referred in the opening pages of my own history of Kent, described the house most lovingly in his autobiography. Mr Arnold has found a diary kept for several years by one Richard Hayes (1725–90) and on the domestic and outdoor intimacies of this record he has written a book which enchants the reader with a touch of historical imagination, ready to walk back into the past, and to savour its perfume, which is not one of decay, but of timelessness, and the sweet honour of English freedom.

SEEN FROM BELOW

I OWE ANOTHER debt to my small dog, a stump-legged Corgi with eyes twelve inches from the ground. We were out strolling together. At least, I was strolling, and he was coursing around, quartering the lane; hedgerows, cornfields, hop-gardens and apple orchards beyond the two hedges. From time to time I was recalled from my meditations (for such is my habit while walking, there being no traffic in the near neighbourhood of the house), by a frenzied yelp from my now distant companion, who had sighted a rabbit. His lifelong ambition has been to catch a rabbit, and he has pursued this purpose for ten long years (equivalent to seventy human years). But so far he has got only within sniffling distance of even the youngest and most innocent bunny. Many is the thud of a warning scut which I have heard in warren and meadow, as the Corgi, never learning by experience to hunt with any degree of sagacity, has rushed headlong in pursuit of the milky-eyed masticators who latterly have learned to wait until he is almost within touching distance before they operate their field-telegraph and vanish in a team. I take his yelp to be one of disappointment, a cry of accumulating and lifelong frustration. Back he always comes, pretending that he was not interested, and that this was merely an exercise in sprinting.

On this particular occasion, however, he did not come back. I heard him across a field and down where it sloped to a brook. There was the usual yelp. But it did not stop. It rose to a different cry, one of pain and then of abject fear.

My meditation snapped off abruptly and I ran up and down the lane looking for a way into the field. The hedge was four feet thick, and reinforced with wire, and stakes in the gaps. The cry was repeated and sustained, and I began to sweat, although the evening was cool. Finally I took off my coat, and pushed it before me through the hedge, at a place where I found two stakes broken away. Bramble and eglantine parted before me, and the cruel spines of the hawthorn. The coat saved my face, but from one or two back-lashings of briar sprays I caught some feline scratches on hands and wrists. And an ankle suffered too.

I was across that field like a hare, following the appeals for help, which by now were continuous and terrifying. 'Where are you?' I shouted involuntarily, wasting my breath as I ran. 'Where are you? Where are you?' I reached the bottom of the field, to find a copse guarded by another hedge this side of the brook, and a weathered and time-twisted thicket of barbed-wire. The cries came from somewhere along this barricade. To and fro I ran, calling to my little friend, while his voice, failing with exhaustion, replied intermittently, with whimpering touches that went to my heart.

At last I found him. There he was, wedged down hind-forward into the entrance of a burrow, with two strands of rusty wire turned round his shoulders where he had tried to double back out of the hole. He was some four or five feet through into the thicket, and I could not reach him from outside. What could I do? The ground was sodden after prolonged rain, and the brook on the other side of the deep hedge was running muddily, carrying down twigs, leaves, bits of decayed wood. There was no way for me to get to the Corgi except by lying flat and wriggling along under the almost impenetrable hedge.

'Quiet now,' I said. 'Quiet, old man,' trying by a touch of authority and discipline to re-assure him. He had seen me. His eyes gleamed like two black agates in the dusk under the bushes. He was shuddering and whimpering still. But my command appeared to soothe him, for he stopped his outcry and waited, his glance following me with that intense semi-blindness which dogs show when they are fixed on a purpose.

My coat came to the fore again. Like Walter Raleigh, I laid it across the wet earth, lay down on my belly, and began to make my way, slug-like, inch by inch through the comparatively open space between the ground and the bottom growth of the thicket. From time to time I paused, put forward an arm, hoping I had got far enough to grasp the captive and release him. But I was never far enough, and the process had to go on, with mud accumulating over my person, and the water soaking into my clothes.

At last I could touch him. He licked my hand. That response moved me almost to tears. 'Steady now,' I whispered. And he waited for me. Within another minute I had taken firm hold of him, lifted him gently round and was able to unwind the vicious wires. His response was a bark of triumph, and a rush toward the shelter of my prone body. There we lay together, a muddy pair.

Now I had to get out. But it was not so easy, for all the loose adversaries which I had pressed back, were now in a superior tactical position for attacking me in the rear as I tried to back out. And they pressed that attack. I paused to consider; and in considering, I looked about me, to realize that for once I was looking at the world from below, from Corgi height. It was transformed.

The little stream was now more than a stream. It was the

River Amazon, roaring down between a vast flanking of jungle growth. Towering out of sight stood here and there the boles of trees whose trunks were lost in a welkin of sombre green. Green was all about me. I breathed green air and touched green water. This was indeed a Marvell-world, with everything reduced 'to a green thought in a green shade'. But they were somewhat intimidating thoughts. To be thus, suddenly, plunged into a tropical exploration, out of the almost sedentary calm of an English lane, was to be taken unprepared. Such is human weakness. I know I ought to have been prepared, on the precept of living dangerously. However, within a moment or two I had the situation in hand, and could begin to appreciate the advantages of my prone position, where I lay flat on waterlogged ground, clasped by a thousand demon vegetable arms, soaked and caked by puddle and mud, with a trembling dog snuggling somewhere about my person under a confusion of garments.

Yet I was happy. The danger past, I could now look upward from this novel angle, to discover the world afresh. Size and position changed their meaning. A fern close to my head became a carboniferous growth out of the coal-forests myriads of years ago. A drooping spray of bramble, with a chandelier of bloom at the end of it, was a great canopy of mauve material capable of shading me through a full-moon of slumber under a lunatic night. A rat plunged into the stream not far from my prone body, and the whole Amazon took the ripples as the monster swam across, ignoring my presence. A hen blackbird, in her rusty coat, set up an alarm above the back of my head. She too was an out-size exotic, blotting the patch of sky which I glimpsed beyond her when I turned half over and saw her.

This was to be in Dean Swift's lands, both Brobdingnagian and Lilliputian, for as my imagination turned from one point of view to another, so I could imagine the smallest weed, the speck of dust, magnified; or conversely the whole world dwarfed to the compass of this patch of woodland and meadow-fall. All depended upon the point of view, and that itself was self-contradictory, and in both aspects utterly strange. I was looking at the universe from below. But what I saw was still a matter for marvelling, for wonder, and for worship. I had my Corgi, and his inquisitive habits, to thank for that.

SMOKE

FROM MY HIGH window I can see smoke drifting eastward through the valley. I try to keep myself attached to the task in hand, but from time to time I have to get up from my desk and to stare out at that pearl-white procession moving like the minute-hand of an old clock, or like the moon rising above a hill; slowly, sedately, inexorably. Smoke from the bonfires burning the hop-bines in the enclosures along the slopes on the opposite, the northern side of the valley; that is the mundane cause of that wonderful pageant. I have seen it year after year, at the end of autumn, when all the leaves are down, harvests in, vagrant pickers cleared out of the huts and settlements, and their rubbish finally cleaned up and piled upon the great heaps of bine-stems gathered like coils of wire. Yet I never fail to marvel at the spectacle, and to wonder how a mere process in the farmers' routine contrives to take on the quality of an oblation, a ceremony, filling the landscape with a sense of awe, and the heart of the onlooker with a certainty of beauty.

Perhaps the silence of it has some authority in the scene. This morning there is no wind. The long east to west valley lies at peace. Sometimes, when a gale is blowing out of the

37

Channel, with the whole Atlantic behind it, this valley becomes a demonic trumpet, through which the Shelleyan south-wester roars and rages like 'old Triton blowing his horn'. Twice I have had the roof torn off my work-room, and I have seen beech trees up-ended, their root clots standing in the air like gigantic mushrooms.

Today the silence is uncanny. I feel as though my ears are plugged with wool soaked in the unguents of sleep. A tiny mist, thread-thick, is laid along the bottom of the valley, an emanation from the stream that winds its way out to join the River Medway farther north at Yalding, the birthplace of that Kentish poet, Edmund Blunden, whose serene verse contains the very essence of this countryside.

As day broke, I went out to watch a thin sliver of sickle moon, which hung below Venus in the southern sky. Below them, and eastward, the sky changed and flushed, silhouetting the hill-ridge and the line of forest. Suddenly two or three trees appeared to step forward, majestically. This illusion was caused by the uprush of light behind them. Then the rim of the sun appeared, and I saw it thicken, rise, until a half-circle of crimson glory, dusted with morning, stood behind those few trees, which I could now see were pine trees. Close at hand, in a cedar, a missel thrush began to shout his habitual defiance, great cadenzas of bravado. Somewhere, unlocatable, dim, distant, and hoarse, a cock crowed, and was answered by one even farther away, a mere ghost of acceptance, no challenge at all.

Since then, with the sun climbing out of that woodland limbo and turning to liquid fire in an inverted dome of porcelain blue, there has been hardly a sound to break the silence of late autumn. One or two robins have been twittering; but their songs are only an accentuation of silence, so tiny, so lonely are their trills and turns. An occasional clatter of holly leaves against each other has proved, but inconclusively, that the air is in movement through the valley. But that miniature traffic dies away as soon as it arises, leaving the landscape even more locked and immobile.

This is the setting for that procession of the smoke. Four or five fires are stages close together, and from each of them rises first a tall, thin column of pearly-white. Then, simultaneously, and with precise gestures, they all spread into a canopy that slowly, almost imperceptibly, loses its millstone solidity and form, moving out eastward, pear-shape, the thin end gradually drawing away above the line of the stream, dropping its fringe as it goes, curtaining the scene immediately behind it, and half-veiling farmhouses, orchards, standing cattle, hop-gardens where the poles are stacked like wigwams. The wisps of fragrance catch and twist in these immobile obstacles, touching them with fantasy. Where one strand of the processional vapour (it is too tenuous to be called smoke) momentarily thickens, it acts as a mirror, passing behind a Frisian cow and reflecting it, so that for a few seconds I see the patient beast doubled against nothingness.

From the source of the pageant, billow after billow leaps up, instantly to be checked in its impetuosity; so instantly that there is a kind of traffic-block about twenty feet from the ground. The ghosts stand still, in their shadow-finery. Then, at a reduced pace, they begin to move up and round, joining the eastward drift, each pulse of whiteness taking to itself some vagary of tint, shape, divergence. Were I a medieval man, steeped in superstition, I might expect to see strange mounts riding these billows, for so many of them have a passing likeness to heraldic steeds; a unicorn, a lion rampant, an armoured horse. But all silent; all stealthy as they pass, pass, pass, tearing their own shapes to tatters through the tree tops, sometimes joining again to make diminutive forms that might be sea birds caught wing-side against the light of the sun, who is now standing in the south, too bright to be gazed at; a vast Presence in space, forbidding human eye to look direct at his glory.

What has happened to the world of men? Somewhere in this scene woodlanders are at work, labourers are trimming hedges, cleaning ditches, harrowing ploughed ground, mucking out farmyards. Farther afield there is the traffic of the modern world, coming and going between villages, towns, single farmhouses and cottages. Children in country schools are chanting their sums, and shrieking in the playgrounds. None of this activity, the mortal stuff of history in the making, comes to my ears. Noon approaches, and soon folk will be knocking off for the midday meal, jumping on to bicycles, tramping up the lanes, slamming the doors. But not yet. The human race has disappeared from the face of the earth. I begin to doubt whether it was the hand of man that lit those fires. I might well suspect that this stately billowing of cool, cobalt-tinged snowiness is the funeral aftermath of the departure of mankind to some other planet, leaving a world of which it despairs, to seek a new beginning freed from the consequences of its old mistakes, its disastrous passions. I am the forgotten one, the sole survivor, left perhaps to tend the last rites, and finally to rake the ashes, for fear the universe may take fire, and the stars be consumed.

It is a solemn realization. I take the responsibility with all the imagination of which I am capable. But I know that my faculties are somewhat numbed by the awe with which they are roused. Is this valley really an Eleusis, where the mystery of the end of the year is proclaimed, with silence to seal it? I think of the Greeks at their rites, practices learned from farther east, and more ancient civilizations. I begin to understand the attitudes of all those vanished races; their worship, their propitiations, and their hopes.

That is the key word, of course; hopes! For where there is a last rite, when conflict and labour are over, when defeat is accepted and despair has come down like annihilation, then there is an assurance that hope is not dead. For if it were, what would be the significance of a final ceremony, a gathering up of the remnants of the human endeavour? What would be the purpose in piling the hop-bines, kindling them, and setting the grand pageant of smoke in process? For this last rite is performed with a purpose, the purpose of cleansing. And where man sets out to clean his land, his heart and his mind, then he is preparing for another adventure, and a new beginning.

As I look out again, leaving my chair for the window, I see that the sun has changed the ghostly smoke to an armoury of silver. Now the procession has its spears toward, and its banners raised. And the missel thrush has begun to shout again, blowing his triple-sounding trumpet, 'Prepare! Prepare! Prepare!'

D

ONE THING I most enjoy about the equinoctial days of spring and autumn in Kent, is that I can rise with the sun and share his sudden monopoly of light. Life being so full and busy, I dare not wait for him on winter mornings. I have to stumble out of bed some two hours before dawn, stirred by owl-cry; or, if I have a particular engagement, by alarm-clock; and I am busy with small rustic duties about the house and barn, and have settled them satisfactorily long before the east breaks and the stars grow pale. As for sharing the solar levitation in midsummer, I think the less said about that the better, though I have the valid excuse that my beaming companion keeps me up so late at that time of the year, that I am justified in lingering after him next morning, in spite of the fact that he is considerably my senior in point of years.

This habit of getting up just before daybreak has made me realize how fortunate are those people whose occupations oblige them to leave their beds 'before Apollo mounts his shining car and shuns the eastern gates'. I think with envy of the milkman, the postman, the drivers and conductors of early buses and trains. They are members with me of what may almost be called a secret society whose ceremonies take place before breakfast, in an atmosphere hushed with joy and expectancy. No wonder that the milk is often deposited on my doorstep to the accompaniment of a flute-like whistle and a jocular 'Chi-hi' to the Corgi who is already sitting outside contemplating the feathered scavengers at work in the lane.

You see that I am trying to treat this matter in a traditional essayist's manner by affecting a mildly jocular mood. In fact, I am casting about as I write, seeking words that shall help me to share the excitements, the revelations, the

42

intimacies which never fail to come every morning when I grope my sleepy way about the twilight world, recognizing one by one the signs of new animation and promise of another active day. The very air is different then. Time stands still for awhile, in a sort of hushed expectancy, before 'out of night Earth rolls her dewy sides', and in that pause the human imagination turns inward to such a depth of insight that it stares into the very heart of all living, all harmony and that superb articulation of time, space, matter and spirit which is the very physical presence of God, for us to appreciate with our five senses.

That is indeed a moment! Even on dull, cloudy mornings, with rain slashing down in the darkness, or a northern fog muffling the world, there comes this period when the aspect of things pauses. One feels that universal hesitation, that look before the leap, and recognizes it as a kind of thought-process of mother nature, as she makes her decision, then rouses the rosy king of light and sends him up to open his wide audiences for the myriad upon myriad of petitioners who are awaiting him.

It affects the machinery of our human thought. I know from long experience that to share in this moment of nature's exquisite indecision before dawn, is to be initiated into a new faculty for insight. It is the hour of intuitions, when problems solve themselves, and worries are dissolved. I have gone to bed at night to toss upon a mattress of uncertainties spiked with misgivings, wide-eyed through the small hours (how wrongly named are those dark periods at the nadir of confidence!), to get up thankfully at my usual time, though still casting about in my mind for certainty and the self-council of right action. Then at that moment just before the rim of the sun appears (or does not appear, according to the state of the sky) I am suddenly taken by a kind of exhilaration of spirit, and I know that I am in the presence of that revealing power which the prophet called 'the still small voice'.

It is an experience about which one cannot readily speak. Like all the fundamental elements of life, it is indivisible and therefore unanalysable. But I can, I hope, share it, for it is universal; it has no price. It is like mercy. But I can recall some of the things it shines upon. I think of the first bird who breaks into song of a March morning. Almost before the dark has begun to thin away, the robin is flitting about the bushes, soliloquizing aloud, so busy with his little musical activity that it sounds like a continuous stream of twitterings. It is a singularly clear and sweet matutinal, and is a most suitable greeting for the day because it is so expressive of hope, busy-ness, and getting-on-with-the-job. Here is no time waster. With his red vest crossed tightly over his ample chest (like Mr Micawber) he is buttoned up for action, and that cheerful obligato from his tiny silver whistle is only another device to hasten things along so that he shall be sure of arriving first in the field, and catching the worm.

That is one voice. Another is that of the barnyard cock. He works on a system of native-telegraph. Startling me out of my still somnolent musing by a sudden outburst of defiance near at hand, from the woodman's cottage in the cherry orchard, the first cock is answered by a slightly more distant neighbour across the lane. The message loses no time; it is passed on almost before the last notes from the second transmitter have died away. As it goes through the countryside, farther and farther into the twilight distance, the sound takes on the chill and huskiness of the hour, until the challenges from the outposts of the coming day sound faint and icy cold like the fairy recollection of Roland's horn, blown at Roncevalles in the Dark Ages, when every dawn was a signal of dangers and extinctions.

Then comes the more jubilant music, after this faintly sinister and admonitory round. It is the joint efforts of the thrush and the blackbird. The first is immediately recognized by his repetitions. Every phrase of his greeting to the sun is triple-sounded, and this gives it an emphasis about which there can be no mistake. The blackbird, that 'ousel-cock so black of hue, with orange-tawney bill', depends entirely upon a contralto majesty to give his phrases their full authority. What a herald! I know of nothing more ample in the whole bird-minstrelsy of England. His oboe-tones take me by the heart, and I stand entranced in my solitude, longing to share this treasure yet grateful to be alone with it, on the shores of day, with the great billows of time already beginning to roll toward me, powerful with the future cradled in their gigantic liquid muscles.

By this time, the sun is up, or the clouds are fully flooded with light, and the ecstatic moment is past. Life begins to teem. Ants scurry about the floor of earth, and all things that move and sound in chorus rather than solo, are now in voice. I fancy I can see the crocuses beginning to open, like shutters being thrown back. From up the lane the sound of humanity is to be heard; a door bangs, a boot scrapes, somebody calls to somebody else. The traffic of the commonplace has begun, and I rejoin the crowd, taking my place with my fellowmen for another working day.

WHEN I THINK of the seventeen thousand new books published every year in England alone, I regard it as a miracle that I should be compelled, from time to time, to pick one out and to be forced by my own eagerness of pleasure to talk about it as though it were a tangible reality in my life. Yet that does happen. I recall that I wrote some years ago about a book of that kind. It was John Masefield's account of his early years, when he worked in a carpet factory in New England. Something in that book was as real to me as the daily events in my own house, and amongst my family and friends.

I have just met another book that has repeated this experience. I must therefore share it, before I return to my usual themes of personal experience on the dusty stage of Europe, where at the moment so many feet are stamping in an act that I cannot properly distinguish as an expression of rage or gaiety.

The book is a short one; merely a collection of essays, notes, observations, sprinkled with a few poems, like snowflakes on a warm sleeve. The writer is a woman: a Welshwoman, married and with a family that occupies her almost to the full. Apart from that 'almost', she contrives to continue with an old friendship for the art of letters, sharing it with her own affairs in so close an intimacy that she brings the reader too into the confederacy, making the personal universal, and by the marvellous paradox of her gentle art consolidating her privacy of spirit by imparting it to her readers. I am sure they will be many: quiet folk like you and me, who do not disguise our bewilderment at so many of the manifestations of the modern world; its noise, its haste, its unrest, its unconscionable fears.

The name of this Welshwoman is Eiluned Lewis, and I learn from her book that she spends her life within the three angles of a geographical triangle, proceeding between them as the season dictates, and carrying with her a family that appears to function like a travelling orchestra, making music at every resting place. And the music is the music of peace, affection, quiet understanding, all those unspoken because ineffable relationships and interests which exist among a group of people whose lives are founded on an unquestioned fidelity toward work, and a deep respect for person and circumstance.

This Eiluned Lewis calls her book *In Country Places*, and has illustrated it with drawings by Gilbert Spencer, an artist possessed by an eye that persists in catching life's good humours. The two together have contrived a piece of work whose unity of mood is for everyman's delight. I am trying to show that delight: but it is always more difficult to reveal pleasure than to parade our grievances. That is why international politics are always so vociferous. If only the Foreign Offices of the various nations would send Memoranda to each other, praising this country's pottery, that country's dancing, another country's architecture, *The United Nations Organization* would at once become an unquestioned sodality!

Such a brotherhood is what we all crave for, so that we can then get on with the marvellous process of living: our daily existence, coming and going as we then could over the face of the earth, one long act of worship. But an ideal existence of that kind presupposes something which today is being challenged by so many peoples who hold the illusion that violence and sudden cleavage alone can bring mankind to a fuller way of life. What instantly struck me about Eiluned Lewis's book was that she sighed as she contemplated this mistake. She lives, and writes, in the belief that, as she says, 'continuity of life is something which we value today perhaps more dearly than ever before in the world's history'.

To those who know what that history is, Miss Lewis's quiet understatement will be heart-rending. But it will also be recognized as food for the spirit, to help it along the road which at this stage of world history is particularly rough and uphill.

What is always so remarkable is that in times of crisis and large events, it is often not the great public figures and men of destiny who put their fingers on the sore spot; fingers touched with the gift of healing. It is some private person, content in his or her own affairs, one 'making verse unto a little clan', who by the very closeness and intimacy of that privacy and its interests, contrives to give voice to the craving, the prayer of all mankind, and through that tiny catharsis to offer a way to new understanding and charity of conduct.

Here in this little book is such a voice. But do not expect it to deal directly with public affairs and world policies. It is mainly about such things as an old Welsh gamekeeper, the different flavours of honey, the birth of two goats, a spring day in the suburbs of London, and New Year in the Welsh mountains. It even spends a whole essay on the making of a handbag for the author out of an old side-saddle that belonged to her grandmother. That last is another neat example of the faith in continuity. 'Keep anything for seven years and you'll find a use for it,' is quoted by Miss Lewis as a saying from her childhood. That homily may usefully be applied to things of the mind as well as to the flotsam and jetsam of the household. Let us not break with the past, with human tradition, with the surviving faith, until we are absolutely sure that every ounce of value has been extracted from it. I feel that Miss Lewis should pass that advice on to all people in authority.

But it is inconceivable to imagine her giving advice. She is far too reticent for that; too reticent and too tolerant, though one feels that behind this gentleness of manner lies a most resolute standard of values, one with a root like an oak tree. In this she reminds me of Thoreau, whom she quotes in the Introduction to her book. 'It is as difficult,' she says, 'to be idle in the country as in a city; perhaps more difficult. But in country places the most ordinary task is continually lightened by a sense of spaciousness which makes for leisure of spirit, if not of body, and that, perhaps, is what Thoreau meant by a margin.' Readers will recall that Thoreau said, in *Walden*, 'I love a broad margin to my life.'

That is a revealing phrase by Miss Lewis: 'leisure of spirit'. It holds the secret of happiness. It reminds us that in serenity is strength, the power to cast out fear and to resume a dignity of mind and conduct which are certain to offer a contribution to the river of public relationships; the river that flows down to feed the ocean of world-wide brotherhood amongst mankind.

These are generalizations: but they are substantial enough, for they are founded upon a solid experience of joy: and I count nothing more real than that: joy in recognizing something true, something saturated through and through with a quiet beauty. That is why I have put the reading of this little book among the experiences that are bound to be confused with my own personal doings, today or tomorrow.

In a recent conversation, I spoke about the benefit of breaking away occasionally from the daily routine, especially if one is a creature of habits rather than of enterprise and adventure. Knowing myself to be prone to this universal weakness, I welcomed another invitation which would snatch me away from my study and the peaceful paradise of my southern garden and cherry orchard. I was asked to go northward, and to one who looks towards the sun as a means to maintaining a reasonable warmth of blood, so that human charity shall flow freely in his veins, I have always been reluctant to venture farther north than Soho Square, or at most the heights of Hampstead which guard London from the Polar Onslaught.

But the suggestion that I should go to Edinburgh, to me that almost fabulous capital of a romantic country always associated in my mind with the dynasties and fortunes of France, was irresistible. Accordingly, with all the temerity of a recluse, I booked sleeping-berths on the train for the outward and return journeys.

Now I am convinced that to travel overnight by train is to arrive at daybreak at any destination with a sense of wonder and incredulity. The transport has been not only material; it has also carried one through the realms of sleep and the drumming and rocking of the train have taken place only partly on this earth. Thus my one-day visit to Edinburgh was enhanced by this approach and this retreat; as it were framed by dreamland and thus removed from the normal contacts and the rational continuities of my daily life.

Cities, like people, have their personalities. Some are immediately impressive, while others are reticent or illusive.

50

London, my own birth-place, is of this last kind. I have known her all my life, earned my bread in her labyrinth, lost my heart and found it again under her canopy, but still through more than half a century she escapes me. I should not care to be challenged to make a portrait of her. It is different with Edinburgh. Like Paris she comes upon one with an instant determination, her character and features concise and unified. I left the railway station at seven-thirty in the morning, a cold but sunny April morning, and I saw the great rock beyond Princes Street and the Castle carved like agate against a sky of soft and misty blue. That hardness and finality of texture gave the key to this whole symphony composed of stone and human history. I stared for some moments and then looked farther around to see that same character of austere beauty stamped upon the whole range of visible buildings, both along the famous Princes Street and upon the heights to my left hand where the old town stood silhouetted like an extended fortification down from the Castle to Holyrood Palace.

This first aspect, so uncompromising, would have terrified me had it not been touched also with an accompanying quality of quiet dignity, which I could only translate as patience. I was to discover more of this during the day, for before I left that night I was to be taken to the heart of that queen of cities and to hear it beating with a tenderness which I shall never forget.

I found from the beginning of my day's adventure that hospitality in Edinburgh is an art practised with both a consciousness and a gesture. A room was put at my disposal in one of the big clubs and a breakfast party awaited me. From that first contact I was fastened to a chain of unexpected and delightful ceremonies which finally landed me at somewhere near midnight in my sleeping-berth on the train returning southward. Amongst them was a visit to the Royal Library where my host, the Keeper, produced rare editions and manuscripts, amongst the former a *Kilmarnock* Burns, an edition which was a model of late eighteenth-century typography, and amongst the latter a letter written in formal script by King Charles the First of England, when he was a child of seven, in which he addressed the King as 'Sweet Father', and proceeded to inform him that 'this day I have three new verbs and seven adjectives', a piece of news that must surely have pleased his Pedantic Majesty King Jamie. Manuscripts of poems by Burns and Walter Scott gave me that sensation of awe and baffled imagination which so often possessed me in youth and I am thankful to confess have not quite deserted me in later life. 'And did you once see Shelley plain?' asked Robert Browning. The question is pertinent to all the higher sensibilities, and if it means nothing to us we are in a poor emotional condition and need a tonic of reverence.

I was taken also to visit a scholar and an artist who were lodged in one of the old stone mansions in the Royal Mile, that almost sinister hill of medieval houses now mostly falling into ruin or inhabited by squatters in slumdon. These two people, however, were determined to bring back into the pride of Edinburgh this street that once was the proudest of its thoroughfares, leading from the Castle to the Palace, and housing the nobility of Scotland when they came to Court from their various feudal glens. It was reminiscent of Montmartre and the Latin Quarter of Paris in the days of Henri Murger, when Mimi's little hand was cold, and Trilby rebelled in vain against Svengali's domination. The view from the rattling windows of the stone-walled rooms was superb, for I looked down from almost Castle-height across Princes Street to the Firth of Forth and the heights of Fife beyond. In the scholar's room I saw evidence of his way of life: the significant confusion of books and manuscripts spilling everywhere, over furniture and floor: the plate of oranges which the sunlight glossed; the cold tea-pot and the stagnant ashtray, whose top dust has blown across the pencils and papers littering the table. I felt that all this was the signature of Edinburgh, symbolizing its life, its reputation and its lasting character: a city of cold endurance, cased in stone but with a gleam of light on a succulent fruit; the husk of the north round an importation from the Mediterranean. Here was France and the past association between Scotland and the South of Europe; an association carried on over the head of unobservant Anglo-Saxondom. So much of Edinburgh reminded me of Paris in this way; the little alleys, the high houses given over to tenement dwelling; the physical discomfort side by side with the high mental adventure.

I found myself, even while lecturing to a friendly audience that evening, looking out from the windows of my active self and seeing before me this powerful personality of a whole city. It was observing me, silently and with an ancient glance, and I found myself compelled to put out my best, not only as a vindication of my Englishness, but to show that I appreciated this neat, austere and wholly preserved civilization so concisely summed up in the Rock, the Castle, the Palace, and the stone streets of Edinburgh.

A NEW YEAR WALK

IN WHATEVER PART of the world I have been, I have
noticed one thing common to all: it is that hardly anybody
who lives in the country goes for walks in it. I know, for
myself, that when I first left Town as a young man, for
reasons of health, I was so entranced by my surroundings
(having been a town-born-and-bred animal), that I could
hardly contain myself within doors. I used to be off and away
as soon as I returned from my daily work in London, only
stopping for a meal after the fatigue of wage-earning and the
daily journey down by train.

In those rapturous years of first-love for the country, I
wandered about like a young Wordsworth, entranced by
everything in general, and by every small object too. The
wind among the woods, the light upon the hills, the cloud-
shadows moving over the plains like the signature of thought
across a human face: these were vast claimants upon my
attention. So were the tiny features of the countryside: the
beady eye of a squirrel or a field mouse, the strut of a robin,
the suspicious lurching of a fox across a glade, the lacy addi-
tions of frost round the edge of a fallen leaf, the bloom upon a
sloe fruit. Large and small, the references gathered in their

54

millions. I was like Ali Baba in the cave, not knowing which way to look because of the myriad riches. A happy state in which to live. I can still remember, how many decades later, what Wordsworth called:

'Those walks well worthy to be prized and loved.'

But that does not last, any more than the habit of the newly infatuated lover who takes to lingering near the house of the beloved, and staring up at the shadow on the blind so cruelly drawn over the window of her room. Living in the country, day after day and night after night, is after all the equivalent of marriage. It calms one down. It brings certain acceptances that need no demonstration. After all, the drawn blind has been lifted, and the intimacies have somewhat altered the relationship. How much deeper it is; how infinitely richer in knowledge and understanding! We have to remember this when we are inclined to say of country-born folk, farmers and their workers, that they do not appreciate the country, and have no aesthetic comprehension of it. They are part of it. Do they need to exclaim aloud, even if they are capable of doing so? It is not so easy to express those emotions, and those reactions even deeper than our emotions, which are a fundamental part of our birthright. We take them for granted:

'I only know
Though all men of earth's beauty speak,
Beauty here I do not seek
More than I sought it on my mother's cheek.'

That is the attitude of the countryman. It is the attitude also of the townsman, like myself, who after the first, fine careless rapture of life in the country, settles down to a rural habit, learning that appreciation is not so satisfying a thing as communion. And work is communion. To work in the country, patiently learning the character of our mother earth, in all her manifestations through the four seasons; that is the real intimacy and the purest and most abiding love.

When, however, we get to this stage, what I would call the connubial stage, we find ourselves so willing to serve that we have less and less time to observe! Certainly we begin to stay upon our own acres, and to wander more infrequently abroad to gaze at wonders and new delights. So it has been with me during the past year, and indeed many years. I found, during the Christmas vacation, that when some of the home-come members of my family suggested a long walk, I was surprised, nonplussed. To my own amusement—and slight chagrin—I found myself saying, 'But where shall we go?' How much change of habit and state of mind were reflected from that one word 'but'. The doubt implied; the loss of recollection; the damped-down ardours! I recognized all the significance even as I said it. And I rebelled for once against the happy humdrum into which my relationship with the countryside had cooled. I took my visitors for a New Year walk, as though making a resolution.

How magnificently was I rewarded! The morning was a brilliantly sunny one. After two weeks of snow, sleet, fog, every dismal contrivance that nature can think up in midwinter, suddenly a dawn came with the sun rising not in sulky red, but with a burst of light that came up over the woods and thrust itself with almost explosive effect over the landscape. Pine trees shook themselves free of gloom, and their trunks glowed red. Sodden lawns turned to Venetian velvet, and the damp woodlands, where mist had smouldered for weeks, stood clear and bold, wide blocks of colour in umber and tawny.

Every living thing responded to this mood of gaiety. As we walked, we seemed to summon out one reception party after another. Missel thrushes, sitting on topmost twigs, shouted a welcome, and triple-sounded it lest we should overlook their hospitality. A lark here and there in the sky shook its song and its wings simultaneously, as though to get the ague of winter disentangled. A flock of finches, rushing out and over, out and over, following down the hedgerows after the falsely roused ephemarids, appeared to be escorting us with a chatter and excitement that got into our blood and made us want to shout aloud some encouragement, meaningless but heartfelt.

And that sky; as blue as the south, and all our dreams of the south, dreams of northern folk whose destiny it is to spend so much of their lives under the wrong canopy (to borrow a phrase from *Coriolanus*): the canopy of grey and obscurity. It was a Mediterranean sky, deep blue, with gentle gradations of pearl and pastel down to the horizon. That alone was a music to our eyes, after the glooms of so many sombre weeks at the year's end. Against this background of blue every hill-top was a clear-cut line, a pencil-stroke of genius. Distant trees and clumps of woodland stood distinct, taking a double meaning through their paradox between substance and clarity. It is impossible to express these things in words, though the poet spends his life and laborious days trying to do so. What a matter for humility, indeed, to think that one short winter walk, taken upon impulse in this way, by a country-dweller long used to the manifest of nature, should reduce his spirit to silence; to an expectancy and recognition which, in concert, have once again roused him to that youthful rapture of forty years ago, a condition of natural worship in which the smallest object has revealed its symbol of eternity.

E

WHEN THE CUP RUNNETH OVER

THE RELATION OF moods to circumstance is something which always fills me with wonder. Long life, and the greater accumulation of experience, still do not serve to explain these contours of our landscape of the emotions. I have been thinking much about it lately, owing to the sudden break in the long-drawn-out winter weather. When March ran wet and bitter, we took it as a morose turn of the season; but when we went south to Italy during April, and wandered about there in mufflers and greatcoats, we began to be occupied with a sense of grievance, sitting outside the cafés drinking rain-diluted cups of expensive coffee and longing for a northern fireside. 'Never mind,' we consoled ourselves, 'it will break soon.' But it did not.

We returned to an England still almost bare of leaf, and even by Whitsun the woods were only half clad, in a kind of transparent vest of green. The processes of the garden were halted, for the cold wet soil could not be touched with spade

or hoe, for fear of puddling it. Every day we examined the
vegetable plots, where the winter-dug clots were dissolved
into a sort of treacly slime marked with the imprint of magpies' feet. There was no other sign of life, except for an
autumn-sown row of broad beans.

Yet for some un-reason or other, I found myself consoled
with hope, and I worked away in the greenhouse with the
consolation there at least of shelter from the inclement weather,
enjoying a few cubic feet of simulated summer. Standing
there one day, while the rain dribbled down the panes and
changed the outside world to a deliquescent jelly, I recalled
one day during the Italian trip when for once the sky lifted
and the sun came out to fill the garden of the ancient villa of
the Medicis, at Fiesole, which a friend had invited us to
view. A long bed of what the gardener called ranunculas, but
which I should have called anemones, made a huge slab of
colour like a Russian salade, under an ancient terrace wall
where a bomb had fallen during the war and brought down a
mass of balustrading. The debris was now draped in a blush-
tinted clematis that stood out against the crumbling masonry
like a young girl against the Muse of History. At the end of
the terrace and the flower-bed of which the gardener was so
proud, a grove of ilexes made a covered path of mossy green
that led to a group of statuary half lost in the dusk of the
avenue.

I could see the figures lurking there, the marble streaked
with mildew; a sad sight, indicating neglect, vanished
grandeur, and faint echoes of *fêtes galantes*. Turning from this
melancholy reminder of the past, I gazed out across the plain,
where the City of Flowers, fair Florence, lay like a huge
cameo carved in rose-coloured stone. Domes, campaniles,
pantiled roofs shone in the sun, faintly misted by distance, so
calm and still that I might have dreamed them. Were they
really substantial, these faint petals dropped upon the wide
Italian landscape? I could only half believe it, though I had

come up the hill from that valley, and had spent day after day exploring the intimate beauty of those petals of the City of Flowers.

Standing in my greenhouse weeks later, still forced to introspection by the inclement mood of the outer world, I suddenly saw that scene and that moment, with the sunlight of an April afternoon drenching the birthplace of so many men of genius that hardly an alley in the city cannot boast some celebrity. Now what was the procedure of this recollection? Why, with trowel in one hand, a diminutive flowerpot in the other, did I lose contact with the task of transferring a seedling from the tray to its second temporary home?

There I stood transfixed, the excitement growing and growing in my mind as with inward eye, like Wordsworth when he recollected the 'crowd of golden daffodils', I recognized one after another of the architectural features among the buildings of Florence. What was the connexion with my present surroundings? Was it a matter merely of colour, the warm earthen-red pot in my hand perhaps associating itself with the roof of the Duomo? That may be; but even so, the explanation is one merely of a mechanism, and not of a cause and a purpose. To go farther into this experience, is to realize that here is the offering of a gift that is miraculous, a treasure conjured out of we know not where. This inward eye, with which we stare upon these recollections, finding in them more detail and more significance than in the original when in a moment of actual time and in a concrete provision of space, we looked perhaps with a listless physical eye that recorded only a vague and general impression; what is this instrument always at hand to surprise us with its contrivances, conjuring the City of Florence out of a small flowerpot, and offering also a commentary on the vision to enrich it with a deeper meaning and an added beauty?

Science cannot answer, though it has been trying to do so for two thousand years, through the medium of philosophy.

But faith answers it, and with an assurance whose joy is like an incoming tide. We know the answer in our hearts. The more I ponder upon this, the more I find for wonder and that something deeper even than wonder. I look for words to express it, and remain content not to find them. For a definition means a conclusion; and there is no conclusion to this tremendous experience of associated recognition between the living mind and the experiences of the past. The man who stood in his little greenhouse, planting a seedling in a pot, was really engaged in ruling the universe and proclaiming the ascendancy of the spirit, that power which presides over the marriage of circumstance to memory, and the union of time and space. The pot in his hand became a superb cathedral, and the rain-blurred pane of glass was changed into the garden of the Medici, open to the serenity of sunlight.

This is the true wealth. I am not surprised that the Greeks made Memory, *Mnemosyne*, the mother of the Nine Muses. With memory still unimpaired, I stand in authority over my own past, and over all that my imagination can command of the past of the human race, and indeed of the universe of nature. With this power, I am capable of joy (that attribute of Heaven) even when the rewards of spring are delayed, and events are poisoned with treachery. Though the world appears to be empty, yet through the wonder of recollection (which is another name for worship), my cup runneth over.

SINCE THE END of the War, English archaeologists have been concentrating their attention upon the Cathedral City of Canterbury, whose history is world famous. A claim can even be made that Canterbury is older than Rome by at least a century and a half. Romulus and Remus, those wolf-suckled twins, are alleged to have founded Rome in the eighth century before Christ. The old historian Lambarde stated that a Celtic kinglet named Lud Rudibras first built a wall round an encampment by a ford across the River Stour, in Kent, in 390 B.C. These are dates somewhat befogged by the distances of time but we can accept them as rough evidence of the fact that Canterbury was a going concern when Julius Caesar arrived in Britain in 55 B.C. and named the town Durovernum, after the Celtic word *Dur* meaning 'water'. We can therefore believe that Canterbury is two thousand years old.

Recent explorations under the foundations of the city have added to the proof that Roman Canterbury was a substantial civic organization, the centre of a community of mixed blood, which reflected the way of life of Rome. It must have been carried on with some sophistication and not a semi-barbaric primitiveness, as we were led to believe in the school-books that misguided our childhood. It has taken me a long time to disabuse my imagination of pictures presenting naked savages dyed with woad, in conflict with merciless and iron-clad Roman phalanxes, native women and children torn with despair and fear, brutal Roman soldiers rushing, sword in hand, and leaving behind them fire and rapine.

What appears actually to have happened was that Julius Caesar came to Kent as a result of political and economic disagreement with the Celtic people, who had long been in close contact with the Continent and had adopted many of the domestic habits common throughout the Roman Empire. The Greek historian, Herodotus, mentions the British trade in tin as early as 450 B.C. This valuable metal was traded to the Phoenicians, who brought to Britain a great variety of goods including their famous purple-dyed cloth. A road was built from Cornwall right across the country to Canterbury and thence to the coast, along which the tin was carried by pack-saddle. The trade was so well established that the Britons even had a gold currency, a factor which is always a sign of economic stability and a high degree of organized civic life. Thus, in later years, I am trying to correct my vision as I direct it towards the Canterbury that at this moment is being unearthed with such minute care, skill and reverence by the archaeologists.

The site of their activities was prepared for them by the German bombs during what came to be known as the Baedeker raids towards the end of the war, when Bath and Exeter were similarly mutilated. Before the damage, the centre of the city of Canterbury consisted of a congeries of medieval alleys that carried their clutches of ancient shops and dwelling-houses towards the Cathedral, like a close flight of golden and russet-coloured chicks seeking shelter under the wings of the mother hen. From within the town the Cathedral could only be glimpsed at odd vantage points between angles of tiled roofs and clusters of chimney-pots. It was not until one reached the Cathedral Close that the full proportions and beauty of the building could be seen. Beneath this close confederacy of bricks and stone and timber, lay the records of a still more distant past. From time to time, when a drain was being repaired, or a telegraph cable laid, the necessary excavation revealed a fragment of that record. These fragments, however, were sufficient to fill historians and archaeologists with a happy despair, for the riches were so obvious. Obvious too was the fact that it was impossible to explore further, because of the buildings and the vested interests above ground.

One night of war-time holocaust removed those surface obstacles. While the war was still in progress, experimental excavations began in what remained of several of the medieval lanes in the heart of the city. It was quickly discovered that Roman Canterbury was about half the size of the medieval city and was contained within a massive wall, which was built about A.D. 200. Within that wall the buildings appear to have conformed to the standards common to cities throughout the Roman Empire. There was the Forum, or market-place, the Civic building, where the administrative machinery of government was housed, the shops and the villas. Much of the building, especially of ground-storeys, was done in stone, in order to accommodate the Roman system of heating by means of hypocausts. These were a system by which the heat from a central fire in the basement was carried in flues through the floors and up the walls of the buildings. In many of the fireplaces of these hypocausts, deposits of soot are still to be seen. These heating arrangements are further evidence of the degree of physical comfort demanded by the Romans in their daily life. After the Romans departed, at the beginning of the fifth century, heating from a central source by dispersion was to remain unknown, or at least unpractised in England until well into the twentieth century. The intervening fifteen hundred years have hardened this island people to every possible form of indoor discomfort in the matter of draughts, icy stagnations and all the rest of the vagaries of our capricious climate.

The excavations are now in process, and day by day further treasures are revealed. It goes on in spite of the enormous expense, even though most of the work is done by enthusiastic volunteers. Tools and equipment have to be found, and sites have to be cleared of debris, masses of post-war vegetation and surviving floors of concrete. As the funds come in, so the work proceeds. A magnificent Samian bowl was discovered in fragments on the site of No. 47 Burgate Street, and has since been reconstructed by the Ancient Monuments Department of the Ministry of Works. It bears the stamp of a potter of the first century A.D. named Murranus. Possibly he was a Venetian from the island of Murano, where to this day the famous Italian glass industry is carried on. Nearby, in Butchery Lane, another medieval alley, the large part of a Roman pavement in mosaic has been revealed. It is a bold design in black, white and pale umber tesserae, in the manner almost of an Afghan rug. Visitors to the Canterbury Festival will be able to see for themselves these evidences of the imperial glories that marked the outposts of that civilization, which, for once, succeeded in creating a united Europe.

IT WAS MIDSUMMER day. I had been at my desk through the routine hours between breakfast and luncheon, and on the previous evening I had worked there until after midnight. The afternoon was hot, and into the open windows of my room the smell of hay rolled like a full tide glutting seashore caverns. It was like the sea, too, in its elemental force. I floated out on the backwash of that invisible flood; a piece of flotsam, an empty shell.

The sun blazed somewhere above. No human eye could locate it, for the whole sky was a cauldron of fire. Time itself was annihilated by that incandescence, and the hours melted into an illusion of eternity. Maybe it was not an illusion. Could not the light have been so penetrating that it touched my inward eye, giving me for once the true aspect of time, so that I saw the present as it hovers between the past and the future, and recognized it as the all-important *now*, which is always here, and therefore eternal?

The ridge that made the opposite wall of the valley was flattened by the heat, and the outline of trees along the summit wavered and broke, and wavered again into solidity. A mist, but not so much as a sombreness, lay along the valley, where the stream crept among the sallows between the hop-gardens and apple orchards. I looked at those distant signs, and I looked at the manifest close to my hand, the meadow ankle-deep in mown grass, the men leisurely moving about in it, turning it with pitchforks, tossing it up and over, little clouds of pollen rising from each shaken truss. One woman worked amongst the men, a stout old wife in a girlish pinafore. Her arms were massive, and tanned like weathered oak. From time to time she stopped to wipe her forearm across

66

her forehead. Seeing me, she grinned and offered me her pitchfork. She was too hot to speak.

I fell into line with the other men, and within a few yards of space and moments of time (both indeterminate measurements in that sun season), I was an anonymous member of the team, and had been so, it seemed, from the beginning of all harvests, down the years, the centuries. It would have been no surprise had I found myself working along some Saxon strip in the common land round an ancient English village.

But here I bent my back in a present-day meadow, with half a dozen fellows who chatted and joked, talking of their motor-bikes and their television sets; men back from the wars in all parts of the world, home again now and back to the Biblical gesture of tossing the hay. No doubt they were amused at seeing the comparatively pallid desk worker coming down from his mysterious occupation with ink and paper, to work among them at slightly too feverish a pace, because his nerves were not attuned to the slower tempo of bone and muscle. They showed no amusement, however; only courtesy and friendliness. I talked with them too, and the pitchforks moved mechanically, tossing the hay, and throwing up the fragrant dust surviving from the flowered grasses. The sun's fire beat down on us all, and on the hills, pressing into the rocks, so that the very minerals pulsed beneath the roots of the writhing vegetable world. All was living in this light-soaked universe; but the life was regular, reposed, a deep and breathing sleep storing up enormous strength towards some future impulse and destiny.

I watched, as I worked, the shadow of a lofty elm tree in the hedge. It grew slowly longer, and moved round towards me. Some kind of indolent conjecture gathered in my mind, as to when, how, and where the tip of that shadow would approach. I saw it take a declivity in the field, where rabbits had scrabbled a tunnel entrance. The shadow touched that hole, and the hole disappeared, so intense was the conflict between light and dark. Neither had mercy upon the domain of the other. Light was a glare of fiery white, consuming all it touched; shadow was instantly total, likewise consuming all it touched. I watched the creeping scimitar of darkness crossing the cropped ground, until it reached the stout old wife who had squatted where she had been working, to rest while I took over her quartering of the field. Suddenly her head disappeared, and I saw a trunk and two arms, one of them fanning nothingness.

That movement, without meaning because of the caprice of the sun, began to act upon my eyes, and the weary brain behind them. I blinked, and I felt the pitchfork in my hands working away of its own volition, collecting the hay and teasing it out and over my head, though I knew that my arms were doing nothing towards this slow and patient movement. I believe I stumbled. And I believe I heard one of the men warning me not to fall upon the prongs of my fork. He was amused, I knew, that I had been out there for not much over an hour, and was already flagging, while he and his companions had tossed the hay since early morning, through the hours of the gathering fury of the sun. I said nothing; merely tried to pull myself together and to command the pole between my palms. For a time I succeeded, by sheer will-power.

Then gradually the rhythm of the universe began to cradle me again. The shadow moved onward, swallowing the old woman, and depriving one of the men of a leg. I wiped the sweat from my eyes and lenses, resting a few moments while I did so. But the cleared vision did not restore me to a full alertness. The elm tree swayed in front of me, and the hedgerows wavered like a huge caterpillar moving over a leaf. I tried, and tried again to grip the pole that was my nearest contact with reality. But it had no substance in my hands. It was only another shaft of fire, to sear my flesh and then to vanish.

I decided to rest awhile, as the old woman was doing,

though not in the middle of the field. Wading through the hay, I slouched towards the elm tree, and moved along its shadow, feeling my way as though plunged into a cold stream of water. The change of temperature woke me for long enough to help me find a spot under the bole of the elm, and there I stuck my fork into the ground, spread my coat over a swathe of bracken, and sat down.

I sat down. I think I sat down; but now I am not sure of my further movements. The coolness of the shade travelled along my skin and caressed my mind. I could still see the glare of white fire on the acres of mown hay, with the delicate, almost violet-tinted dust rising from it. I lay back against the bole of the tree, pressing softly against a spring of twigs, the new-season growth. I looked up into the green height, and felt my eyes roll beneath the lids, out of control.

Where is that next moment; and what takes place in the human spirit? The philosophers ask and ask, but the problem remains inscrutably removed, part of the universal benevolence of healing, where seeds lie, resolutions are formed, wounds are healed, and knots unravelled. I had fallen asleep.

NOTICING ODD THINGS

I AM NOT sure whether it is a curse or a blessing to be
endowed with a faculty for noticing odd things. I must confess that I am more than half ashamed of myself on those great
occasions (and we all have our great occasions) when instead
of re-acting with some degree of heroic fervour, I find my
attention fixed upon what I know to be irrelevancies. This
weakness began in early infancy, for I can recall that when,
at the age of four, I accompanied my parents to watch the
Royal Procession at Queen Victoria's Diamond Jubilee, I
ignored the martial music, and jingling hussars, the cheering
and the banners. The only thing which took my attention,
and has since remained in my memory for over half a century,
was the way in which the tiny old lady sat in her open
carriage, swinging forward on a spring seat, so that she had
the appearance of bowing to the homage of the crowd. But
her movements were made with such metronomic regularity
that even a child could notice their mechanical origin.

I must be dogged by this habit of slightly facetious ob-
servation, that borders upon irresponsible satire, though I
deplore it, and would gladly dispense with it. But I cannot,
and I begin to suspect that I may be well advised to accept
my idiosyncracy, turning it to good account, as the oyster
accommodates itself to the grain of sand in its shell, working
upon it until it is no longer a fault and an intrusion, but a
pearl of great price.

During the last two days I have needed some such reas-
surance of this. Just as three weeks ago I had occasion to
break my country habits and make a journey to Edinburgh,
so now I have been compelled for professional reasons to come
south (a direction I always prefer). I find myself in Florence,
and during the journey from an England still prostrate under
a prolonged winter, I grew more and more excited as I
counted over the treasury of book memories, gathered
through a lifetime of reading, of all matters literary, historical and cultural, in which Florence has figured, from
Dante's *Vita Nuova* and the primitive paintings of Cimabue,
through the glories of the Renaissance and the Courts of the
Medicis, to the latter-day associations of the Romantic period,
when Florence became almost a sacred plot of English
ground, harbouring such immortals as Walter Savage Lan-
dor, the Brownings, John Ruskin and John Addington
Symonds.

I arrived here loaded with these anticipations, and half
nervous about realizing them. Time had made them so
familiar and so precious. Through most of my life they have
been the accepted furniture of my mind, treasures created for
my private use by the artists and craftsmen who, during the
course of the Middle Ages and the Renaissance, contrived to
make their native city truly a City of Flowers, one of the
most superb Civilities of the world. Hitherto, I had enjoyed
those riches only through the descriptions of critics and
historians, and from mechanical reproductions. Now I was to

come face to face with Michelangelo's *David*, Botticelli's *Birth of Venus* and *Primavera*, Giotto's Campanile and Brunelleschi's Duomo. It was so great an occasion that I was almost afraid.

I had reason to be. Who would not, who has had experience, and has learned through that experience to be conscious of the devious ways by which the human soul approaches its estate? The mind works quickly and with a proud impatience. It wants everything at once, so that it can create understanding from reflections and contrasts, juxtaposing time and space, cause and effect, flattening them into a graph, a map, a deceptive simplicity.

That is how I came to Florence, intending to start at once to test my years of reading by rushing from one monument to another, and exploring the picture galleries in a mood of passionate concentration.

But I had forgotten—as we always forget—that the soul, through its instrument the creative imagination, does not work in that accusative and rational way. It does not challenge things and events. It does not contrast one with another. It goes to work passively, and with a slowness that is part of the rhythm of its great Monitor. It looks out as a child looks out, seeing a little at a time, but accepting that little as something universal and absolute.

We cannot explain this. We rebel against it, because our minds thrive upon explanation, and our intellectual pride comes tumbling down when we find ourselves standing dumb, baffled, naïvely innocent, in front of the spectacle of nature and of man's achievement.

Such has been my humiliation during my first few days in Florence. I have visited the galleries, stared up at Giotto's marble and Brunelleschi's rose-red tiles. I have stood in front of immortal paintings made too familiar by reproductions. I have rushed greedily from one palace to another, where the history of this City of Flowers has solidified in pomp and splendour. And what have I gained from this feverish activity?

I do not know. I have tried to know, but once again the realization has come home to me that in these matters of the fundamental enrichment of the personality, the processes of the spirit's growth, there is no value in hurry. Thus I am aware of one or two humble moments in these days of rabid exploration. I can see already that it is not ridiculous, or an act of *lèse majesté*, to record them; for I believe there is a meaning and a guidance in this.

These, then, are the only wonders that have come to me, to be my own and part of my enlargement. First, I have lain in bed, listening frequently in the night to the tumbling of the waters of the Arno over the weir before they reach the Ponte Vecchio. That night-music must have been familiar to Dante in his youth and haunted his hungry years of exile spent in 'eating other men's bread and climbing other men's stairs'.

Secondly, I have noticed that Florence is a city of swifts. They fill its skies, patterning every clear space between its roofs, and over the length of the Arno, with quick arabesques and a high cry whose shrillness ceases only at sundown.

Thirdly, I have heard, in the Boboli Gardens above the town, the first nightingales to greet my ears this season, jug-jugging and wounding their own hearts amongst the blossom of the wild cherry trees.

And finally, as though to crown the humiliation of my mind after its proud claims to all the wealth of Florentine history and art, I have noticed that the little local cheese, the *Pecorino*, tastes of fresh grass!

These are small acquisitions to take home. But I am ready to accept them as sufficient wealth, as a gardener accepts his seeds, trusting to the future.

F

ALL THE WEEK the clack-clack of harvesters, and the moan of tractors, have supplied the music for the day, and indeed far into the night, for the harvesters have been working by the light of the moon, trying to get the oats cut while the weather has been kind. Happily for the looker-on who loves to see the recurrence of old shapes and customs, the reaper-binder is not much used in my part of England, and we still are able to enjoy the prospect of fields set with stooks after the cutting has been done. I know of no sight more serene. It is like the face of the mother of a family, after her brood has gone out into the world, and she sits at home ready always to receive her children when they are at liberty to come back to her with their achievements or losses.

I have watched the coming and going, for this ceremony of harvesting sets in train a vast traffic, both human and feathered. The machines need attention, and boys set off on bicycles to fetch spare parts, cans of oil and tools. Wives and children meanwhile keep up a shuttle service of supplies in the food line. It is indeed a line, for it stretches all the way from the village to the fields, at least a mile and a half, and the lane is never free of one or more figures toiling along basket in hand. Cans of cold tea are much favoured also, and these come swinging on the handlebars of children's cycles ridden with such high spirits and excitement that it is a wonder the liquid arrives intact.

The weather was kind during the cutting; three days of solid summer, with the sunshine set fair and square in the face of the day, something almost to handle and caress, it was so prominent and pervading. So too was the shadow, a definite object under every tree, and a wall of solace running alongside the hedgerows, where at the stroke of noon from the

74

distant church clock, the workers gathered and set about the job of attending to the various baskets and cans which had been coming along the lane during the course of the morning, and settling in the cool grasses with a jacket, a scarf or a sunbonnet to mark their identity.

The munching and supping was accompanied by no small amount of banter. It is odd how much of the conversation of these countryfolk consists of a sort of gentle irony or satire, at each other's expense. 'Now Jack,' says one, his mouth stoppered with a hunk of cheese, 'did you buy those giddy trousers at a woman's shop or a man's? They look to me like those things the girls wear nowadays!' The other replies, after a swig at his bottle of milky tea. His eyes are twinkling with mirth. 'Naw, Tom! Yer know I borrowed 'em off of my missus! I can't afford to go buying trousers for meself, not with things as they are. Look at the price of tobacco!' Then a third chips in, busy with his clasp knife round a crust of meat pie. 'Yew don't tell me that, Jack! What about that gratuity you got coming out of the army when the war ended? Yew ain't never spent that, I'll allow. Not if I knows your habits.' Jack is a little huffed by that criticism, and he says nothing; only goes on eating with his face a blank mask. Offence is seldom openly shown.

Meanwhile, the fields being quiet and the machine standing silent, the traffic of birds has increased a thousandfold. Flocks of sparrows especially are busy, swooping down like cataracts of brown water, their wings in chorus making a miniature roar as of a tempest. They alight in formation, sweeping up a little, shovel-like, before settling round the sheaves of corn which lie just as they have been dropped by the binder. They keep up such a chatter that surely they have no time to eat. Dodging and prying, they almost tumble over each other, and from time to time two will have an altercation that ends in a savage attack three inches from the ground, wings spread against wings, and beaks clashing. Then suddenly something will signal to the whole formation, and with another roar of wings the birds are off to another part of the field, giving room for a couple of magpies to come paddling down out of the air, their tails lagging behind them as though loaded with lead. Starlings, rooks, and even a few sea birds follow, the latter salted, clean, bleached, in comparison with the softer and fuller colours of the inland creatures. Down the field a cat, adventuring from the nearest cottage a quarter of a mile along the lane towards the village, is sitting, contemplating this feathered activity, her tail slowly lashing to and fro, and her mouth occasionally opening and quivering in a galvanic spasm of lascivious eagerness. But she does not move.

The hedgerows are full of honeysuckle, and the perfume of it blows along the headland, deep, superb, intoxicating to the imagination. All summers past, and especially those of our own childhood, are contained in that scent, which drips its nostalgic riches out of the very air and light. Mingling with it, more immediate in its appeal, is the almond-like tang of the meadow-sweet, proclaiming 'all summer in a day'. Somewhere along the hedge, a yellow-hammer is complaining with his tiny, stammering song, to be answered by another, each with his 'little bit of bread and no . . . cheese!'

What a picture it is; like a serene masterpiece by Brueghal, or our English Samuel Palmer. This prospect of green and gold, with the blue above, and the smouldering flash of wings, the weathered aspect of human faces and forearms, a dog's thirsty tongue lolling out and being made transparent by the brilliant sunlight; all is so saturated with light and heat that one feels it can never change, never vanish.

But it does. Within a few hours clouds have begun to gather unnoticed in the south-west, rising out of the sea between England and France. Then a breeze quietly stirs the scarves lying across the emptied food baskets. This movement is followed by the sudden whimpering of the hedgerows bushes, as they bow their topmost twigs and then suddenly swing down in a gesture of fear. A great oak half-way along the field flaps itself, like a man trying to warm his hands in winter. The wind takes hold of a half-made stook and tumbles it down again, causing the harvesters to look up in surprise at the sky, and to find it piling with masses of leaden cloud.

Everybody follows suit, staring up at the threat that does not remain a threat for long. Within another half hour the first drops fall. A flash of artificial fire flickers out from the sulphury-grey centre of this disturbance overhead, to be followed by a growl of thunder. The dog with the long tongue stops panting, looks to right and left in apprehension, then with his tail between his legs, creeps under the shelter of a waggon. Now the men are working feverishly, trying to get the sheaves stooked before the worst happens. Will they do it? The rain is now dripping, here and there, gobbets of water as big as a dollar. Faster the stooping and heaving figures move across the field, throwing up the sheaves so skilfully that each stook stands as firm as a citadel. The rain can now be seen along the hill top beyond the village, a grey mist that is creeping down the slope and will almost immediately be on top of us. Shall we get through? Everybody is hard at it, even the onlooker and commentator! For the corn is everybody's concern; the common property of the human race.

Only one more row to handle! But the rain is pelting, and the lightning has whipped out again, crackling across the stubble and touching a few cornflowers with its blue fire; blue to blue that turns the blossoms into eyes of frightened innocence. The cat has disappeared. Now the birds have gone too, except for a few sparrows, greedy to the last. This is the end. Here is the deluge. Down it comes, foaming and steaming. Suddenly, as by a captain's signal, the humans too are flying before it, disguised under sacks, making for shelter in the open cart shed at the corner of the field.

NOW THAT THE summer rains have lifted, the whole county is on the move, bringing home the harvest. For two weeks or more the corn has waited for the weather, stooked firmly against wet and wind. It has been a sight to conjure courage in the most timid heart, in spite of the threatening skies. Over the contours of the land, this army of golden tents has been bivouacked, waiting, ready to march: an army of opulence, not of destruction.

I have been out, idling away my working hours, watching the waggons, where they stand hove to, or rocking down the fields like King Philip's galleons bringing gold from the Americas. Waggon after waggon, in generous manœuvre, pulled by tandem-harnessed horses (for the slow movement and the frequent halts make the use of a tractor uneconomical) tacks across the stubble, piling up, higher and higher, as the sheaves are thrown on the long-handled forks of the men who trudge beside the splayed wheels, like halberdiers at a coronation; which indeed this adagio ceremony is; the coronation of the year.

Here is a sight for over-hasty eyes, nervously seeking they know not what at the frantic bidding of town-tired nerves. Here is no hurry. So I sit down, like the Spirit of Autumn herself, as depicted by the poet John Keats:

> 'On a half-reaped furrow sound asleep,
> Drowsed with the fume of poppies.'

If not sound asleep, I am resting in a mood of content and a racial thankfulness that lies beneath my conscious mind, down through my ancestry to primitive man, who first sowed a handful of corn, and gathered its hundredfold return with a curved flint tied with thongs to a stick. My attention fastens on the scene, and drifts away again, abandoned to its own surety, for I know this picture is an eternal one, returning so long as mankind survives.

Sometimes I am fascinated by the progress of the waggons, compelled to wonder why the pauses are so long, with the horses standing patiently, sacks over their backs, their tails flicking in curves over each flank to repulse the flies. What are the men talking about among themselves, with distant bursts of laughter, or deep grumbles of sound accompanied by the lighting of cigarettes or pipes in cupped hands, their halberds upright between their arms? This waggon nearest me is loaded to a perilous height, so that a sigh of wind coming up out of the afternoon sets it swaying gently. A boy sits in the middle of it, saying nothing. Perhaps he is drugged by the warmth and the dusty smell of the wheat; intoxicated on future loaves of bread. What is this still-alive scene, this sudden arrest? But before I can answer, the waggon begins to move away, the first horse putting out his hoof like a somnambulist, the shaft-horse shuddering and thrusting from his hindquarters, so that the skin of his flanks trembles and sends the flies off in a cloud. As the waggon moves, the men on each side of it shoulder their forks and stride with stately paces, looking up at the load above them, as it sways, dips, rights itself and dips again. One lurch the more, surely, and it will tumble, bringing the boy with it. But always it recovers, swaying up again and riding the stubble safely.

Sometimes my attention wanders from this land fleet, and I turn to things near at hand, the signs of life and survival in the stubble, where my Corgi is quartering so eagerly, following his nose and jerking it back from time to time as his curious nostrils are pricked by a thistle or a ragged edge of straw. From a distance, the field looks like a mat of bristle, sandy and monotonous in colour. But a closer scrutiny brings more to the eye. Within a yard of me I can see a cluster of

feathers where some small tragedy has taken place, with owl
or weasel as the villain. A wheel has dishevelled a nest, either
of lapwing or partridge, and in the debris of it I can identify
the half of an egg-shell, touched with freckles over a misty
blue ground. A small spider sits within it, nursing his yellow
bag. To my right is the shallow form of a hare, composed of
flattened and miniature teazles dried over two seasons.
Perhaps he was trying to curry-comb himself, perfecting his
red coat as he lay hidden in the standing corn.

A regiment of ants is passing that spot, wearing a small
black uniform, too Lilliputian for me to see their badges. I
needs Dean Swift's lens for that. Where and why they are on
the move I do not know. Nor, apparently, does the huge slug
anchored across their path like a dreadnought. He ignores
them, and they divide and go round him, a file on each side,
rushing along so rapidly that I can suspect them of being
mechanized.

Here and there, splashes of ragwort, flaming yellow,
collect hundreds of butterflies, most of them the tiny meadow-
blues whose wings always look as though the colour has been
rubbed a little, dropping off in azure dust. On a larger scale,
an enormous sow has come through the open gate at the
bottom of the field, and she is followed after a comic interval
by her litter, like peas rushing back into the pod. They are
unlimited, a stream of fecundity. Suddenly the flow stops.
No, there is one more, smaller than the rest. He plunges
squealing into the mêlée round the mother, and is soon first at
the fountain-head.

All this activity, of man and miniscule, is framed in hedgerows set with great sentinel oaks that have stood here for
centuries, watching the processions of harvest after harvest,
and of human history. I look up into the one against whose
trunk my back is supported, and I see a squirrel, his beady
eye abusing me, while his teeth chatter with greed at the
prospect of such ample gleaning.

High above the top-most twigs of the oaks, a jet-plane whistles past, leaving a trail of vapour in the sky. It must be passing from one planet to another, for it can have no possible association with all this traffic of mother earth below. It must have occupants. Do they see what is in process down here; the ancient rites of autumn, the religious procession bringing home the corn, as it was brought home two thousand years ago, when Virgil and Theocritus watched as I am watching today? And if they see it, do their minds, changed by supersonic speed, contrive to understand the seemingly flat, seemingly dead-still map of nonentity?

I cannot follow those questions, for I am sufficiently occupied to answer a thousand more familiar ones which men have been asking themselves year after year, age after age, at every autumn season when the waggons go lumbering and stumbling home with the harvest, heavy with their mystery, loaded with tomorrow's bread.

I WAS CALLED, the other day, from the world's pre-
occupations, and those crowding events which come upon us
increasingly with the years, by glancing at the title of a new
book. Now new books fall upon the attention almost as
incessantly as new eventualities in ones private and public
life, and we acquire a case-hardening process of resisting their
appeal. But this book was called *Peace and Dripping Toast*. It
was written by one Frederick Willis, and that reminded me I
had written before about the London in which that man spent
his boyhood at the turn of the century.

I think I have not even heard mention of dripping toast for
several decades. I have certainly not eaten it since boyhood,
and I suspect that were I to be offered it now I should find
that my palate had lost a certain gusto for that rich, fatty
delight. But as a symbol I welcome it, because it stands for a
period, a way of life, maybe even a particular part of the
world, with which I was familiar in childhood. And always
the scene of our childhood maintains an element of glory, and
of timelessness, which no later experiences can tarnish.

Can I recall that period, that way of life, that particular
part of the world? It will be no easy effort, for all three
aspects of the past are remote in mood and nature from the
present. So much has vanished, and we do not even notice
its going until an occasion, such as my meeting with this
reference to dripping toast, startles us into a consciousness of
comparisons. Nor can I expect readers in far parts of the
world to be able to come with me to the south-eastern
suburbs of London in the year 1900. That is making too
egocentric a demand! Yet it is worth while. Without that
effort, for example, it will not be possible fully to savour the

genius of Charles Dickens; for his immortal tales are full of the odour of dripping toast; sound, round-of-beef dripping with a layer of stiff jelly at the bottom of the basin. And the toast has to be hot, so that the dripping soaks into it.

Dickens knew that flavour! It represents a social reality; the reality of the small man in his millions, still full of idiosyncrasy, whose daily labours based on hope and a tangible ambition, gradually built up the Western World of democracy founded on a reasonable loving-kindness. It is the world which hitherto we folk in Britain and North America have taken for granted as the basis of civilization: a world where a man can think as his conscience directs; can work for himself and his family under that direction; can emerge occasionally from his privacy to assert his modicum of authority in the running of the community, and then return to his dripping toast, his own fireside, his little grumble and his great faith.

Why is this queer item of diet a symbol of a whole way of life? Because it is based on a special economy which no longer obtains. As Mr Willis says in his opening paragraph, 'When I was born the State had few contacts with the individual. People in my station of life rarely received a communication franked *On Her Majesty's Service*. When such a letter arrived they were inclined to preserve it as a philatelist does a rare stamp. When the individual was born the State insisted upon being apprised of the fact. When the individual passed over the State marked him off like a bad debt. But between these two events the State left him to make the best journey he could through life. There were advantages and disadvantages of this arrangement, but it encouraged the development of 'characters', and characters made my world exceedingly robust and interesting. There would be no place today for Uncle Toby and Tristram Shandy's father, but they could have got on very well in the world I remember. It seems to me, therefore, I had the good fortune to live through the last three decades of English individualism.'

Mr Willis lived through those decades in south-east London, not far from the quiet, picturesque village of Dulwich which even today keeps some of its rural character, preserved, I hope for ever, because of the nature of the will left by Edward Alleyn in the reign of James I of England. In 1616, the year that Shakespeare died, Alleyn, famous actor and part-owner of the Globe theatre in Southwark, built and endowed in the centre of Dulwich Village a 'college' for twelve poor boys and an almshouse for twelve old people. He had bought the estate from one Galton, a goldsmith, who had received the land from King Henry VIII in settlement of an outstanding debt which the monarch was not able to settle until after the disestablishment of the monasteries.

Alleyn parcelled out the income from his estate so that each inmate of his foundation should receive a few shillings a week for maintenance. An Act of Parliament had to be passed during the nineteenth century to revoke this will, for the parcels of land were then bringing in to the almsfolk some hundreds a year each! Alleyn also interdicted the felling of timber on the estate of Dulwich, so to this day there are woods and groves there, to remain as an oasis in a wilderness of bricks and mortar. In Dulwich Wood the poet Robert Browning, born at Camberwell Green, wandered when a boy, learning the nature lore that so enriched his work. Dickens's Mr Pickwick, more real than so many flesh and blood people, retired to Dulwich, settling with Sam Weller in a tiny white house, with narrow windows and a high hedge in front of it, opposite a grove of elms called Lovers' Walk, along College Road, only a hundred yards from Alleyn's mellow old almshouses. A famous English 'public' school has emerged from that college, but the original building is intact (badly damaged during the World War). It still has the organ in the chapel, with the white and black keyboard in reverse colours. Handel played on that organ.

But I am losing sight, or rather smell, of that dripping

toast. I ought to go on to an economic analysis of the way in which the near-poor lived in that age of individualism, when as Mr Willis says, the State left us to our own resources, to sink or swim according to our ability, health and courage. We carried on by the exercise of that nineteenth-century virtue called Thrift, less often mentioned nowadays because the significance of its effects has shifted. But dripping toast was the symbol of it. The Sunday joint had to be the cornerstone of that individual economy, and round it the family life was built up. The cooking of that joint produced a bowl of dripping, and in those days margarine was an unknown or at best a despised commodity; while butter at a shilling a pound might be allowed for thin bread-and-butter at Sunday afternoon tea, but not for mass consumption by a hungry young family: eager individualists with open mouths like a nest of thrushes. The State contributed no free milk, no dinners at school, no medicines and tonics, to those gaping mouths. They had to sing for their supper, and it was a song of hard and competitive work, learned at mother's lap and on father's knee, under the direction of a Bible text. And the supper was dripping toast.

BURNING THE BINES

I WISH THAT at this moment I could bring to a certain corner of England all people who love rhythm, shape, richness of design, and invite them to watch the burning of the bines. It is a large-scale ceremony, covering the county of Kent, and it is one of the most beautiful I know. It brings peace to the mind, and serenity to the heart. Why is that? If I knew the answer I should be the greatest artist in the world, for I should know the secret of bewitching humanity and lifting it above the ravages of time and circumstance.

It takes place once a year, in November, at the falling of the leaves and the close of the season. It is thus a ceremony of farewell. The year is behind us, with harvest in and most of the ploughing done. Thus the landscape is already settling down to its winter form, under a quilt of bare fields, moleskin colour warmed here and there to russet by the iron in our soil: those that have been autumn-sown already powdered with emerald dust, that glitters in the winter sunshine, and spears the occasional sheets of snow and frost with tiny blades whose vitality maintains the troops of tits and finches until the earth is bare again. The foliage is tumbling down in bulk, like a woman's cloak being cast off when she comes home weary

86

from a party; all of a heap, its riches and its hues mingled carelessly upon the ground. Through the woods and copses, and along every tall hedgerow (for which Kent is famous), the damp but fiery carpet is spread, with millions of spiders rushing over it trying in vain to stitch its tatters together with their shining silk threads. The colour is there, but it is all subdued under the fall of the year. It is broken colour, of umbers, inky blues and blacks, soaked yellows, and those soft neutral browns that are doomed for perpetual background. What a royal carpet for the feet, commanding reverence by its softness, its silence. To walk in woods now, is to walk in a hushed and holy place. Almost unconsciously the voice is subdued to these surroundings, to whisper with the fallen leaves that susurrate about ones shoes. And the perfume of the leaves! It comes up like the breath of memory itself, all the world a thurifer swung in this last ritual of the seasons.

The countryside changes its habits, its social habits, at this time. The invasion of the fruit gatherers and the hop-pickers is over. The noisy tide of that periodic mass of humanity has ebbed back to the towns, leaving the orchards and the hop-gardens somewhat disordered with litter, as all floods will. The farmers and their men go about methodically to clear up the jetsam, spending a week on the job. They clean out the rows of huts where the hop-pickers have bivouacked for a month or six weeks, and pile up the debris in great mounds. It is astonishing what the city dwellers leave behind: old bedsteads, prams, boxes, broken bits of furniture, discarded radio sets, pots and pans, bolsters, garments: none of it very fragrant. After this unsavoury harvest, the farmhands work their way systematically through the hop-gardens, going up and down between the poles and wires, preceded by waggons, horse or tractor drawn, into which they pile the bines that lie like discarded coils of wire round each 'hill'. A hill is the name for the root of the hop-bine, which is perennial, to be renewed every ten years or so. After the first one or two seasons, the hill becomes a small mound, due to the cultivation between the rows, and the application of fertilizers (shoddy waste from Yorkshire, or sacks of feathers).

The amount of bine is enormous, for hops are prolific in growth, rushing up from their hills with such speed that between April and July they climb some ten feet to the top of the poles and are already fanning out along the overhead wires to make a roof, so that the gardens become huge bosquets where one may walk in geometrical glades, under a green problem in Euclid where every angle becomes a tendril as delicate as a baby's finger. Like Jack's beanstalk, they wax in strength and number, shutting out the sunlight and subduing everything beneath them 'to a green thought in a green shade'.

At the time of the gathering, all this growth, crowned by its bacchic fruits, is torn down so that the pickers can pluck the hops and fill them into 'bins' (canvas hammocks slung between poles on tripod legs). By now the bines are hardened and are about as tractable as telegraph cable. This waste stuff has to be removed from the gardens so that the ground can be tilled and fresh fertilizer spread. Sometimes it is piled in the gardens and burned there. More frequently it is brought out into the open grassland in front of the hoppers' huts, heaped over the rubbish cleared out of those huts, and there burned: a most sanitary process, leaving a heap of potash from which the men carefully sort out the odd bits of metal.

That is the utility aspect of the process. What I want to portray is the aesthetic, I might even say the mystical effect, of the dozens of fires as one sees them scattered over the landscape. But the Kentish scene has first to be imagined; and that is difficult unless one has seen it in actuality. All is so intimate, yet so expansive. The vast Weald, swung by nature between two walls of downland, is a series of undulating patches of richly quilted land, divided by high hedges enclosing strips of colour as gay as Joseph's coat. We see the emerald of newly sprung corn, the umbers of fallow land, the smudges of copse and woodland, now a whole palette of smeared hues. Groups of oasts, like castles in the backgrounds of medieval paintings, cottages, farmhouses and noble manors, church towers built from Kentish ragstone; these give the signature of humanity, if that were needed to emphasize how man has subdued this countryside, during two thousand or more years, to his will and his craft traditions.

All this picture, raised in a delicate superstructure of tree trunk, roof, spire, fencing, hedgerow, and the great squares of bare poles in the hop-gardens, is now to become a sort of notation through which the music of the smoke winds its way, a slow script written under the inspiration of the air, the moving breezes thinking out their patterns as they touch the dense columns of smoke and turn, diffuse, twist and direct them over the Weald, linking and dividing, threading the exquisite strands of ghost-like silver and grey between the solid verticals erected by man and nature. And the smoke moves! It moves like beauty itself; like recollection in the mind of the aged man and woman, infinitely sad, infinitely serene. It becomes a writing, and the words it inscribes upon the face of the earth are 'Peace', and 'Thanksgiving'.

G

A FRIEND OF mine, an excise officer, was travelling in pursuit of his duties in Ireland. He was in a remote part of County Cork, one hot summer day following rain. Weary of the humid heat and the interminable journey, he put his head out of the window to see the time at a wayside station (his watch having stopped). But there was no clock. Nor was there any other moving thing, for the one porter in sight was sitting on a trolley gazing into the blue hills. My friend hailed him, and asked what was the hour. 'I don't know,' said the porter, with a friendly turn of the head and a gracious smile. 'Don't know?' said the exciseman. 'D'you mean you've got no clock in the station, to time your trains by?' 'That we haven't,' said the porter, 'and why should we distress ourselves with time?'

The music of that phrase has haunted me ever since I heard the tale many years ago. To distress ourselves with time! What an occupation; and how many of us, in this world of hustle and bustle, are addicted to that habit! All townsfolk, I suppose, are liable to come to that condition because of the speed of their surroundings. We do not notice the effect upon our consciousness, just as a passenger on an ocean liner does not notice that the whole miniature floating city is hurling itself along at nearly thirty miles an hour. But when we escape from the streets and the traffic, coming to a quiet place, we perceive suddenly that our minds and bodies have been keyed up to a sort of super-concert pitch.

The result of this is always to heighten our appreciation of silence, that deep-dropping silence which soaks through the very fabric of nature, settling down to the placid calm that underlies time and space; a condition which, to our perpetual amazement, we recognize at once with a joy that contains the wealth of the universe.

I know, for myself, that those moments are some of the most welcome in my experience. Every time I come down to my home from London, I renew that experience, and it never stales. The din of the train journey, the car drive up into the hills from the wayside station on the Weald—and then the silence. Ah! It is a substantial thing. It covers the landscape, as personality covers a human figure. The hills are conscious beneath it, the woods and fields are full of it as though it were an underflowing current of life-blood, deep, restorative, cleansing. I stand and look at this invisible presence, before going indoors. And that moment's pause is an act of prayer and thanksgiving.

But when I enter the house, this sudden inheritance enters with me. The country interior is not the same as that of a home in town. The clocks tick in a kind of intense isolation. In a distant room somebody puts down a cup, or coughs, or speaks. It is a distinct event, rounded off, dropped plumb into space, and contained absolutely, like a stone down a well. Depth; that is the quality which is indicated by this tangible presence of the silent universe: and a depth which contains all the past, the present, and the coming riches of conscious life. How impossible it is to define it at all. I seem only to be able to approach it by a series of negatives. It is not in the tempest, it is not in the still, small voice. It lies beneath even that; the universal quiet upon which everything rests. Here indeed we are down to bed-rock, the fundament of reality. And it is an experience that brings joy, the restorative joy in which are contained all power, all faith, all possibility of achievement.

I was reminded of this condition of the spirit, and of that quaint story of the Irish railway porter who could 'not distress himself with time', while showing a French friend round Kent last week. We had been exploring the famous Romney Marsh,

visiting the ancient church of Stone-cum-Ebony, and tracing
the archaic Persian symbols on a Roman altar which now
stands under the tower of the church, after serving for centuries as a mounting block for folk coming to church on
horseback. It was a time-annihilating occupation, in two
senses of the word; a gentle way of passing a summer afternoon in an unfrequented spot; and a leaping back over the
centuries; to strange eras of thought and worship, before
England was a Christian land. The church stands at the
whalehead of a ridge of high land that was once an island
surrounded by sea. The currents in the English Channel have
silted up deposits during the past four hundred years, turned
the course of a small river, and left the port of Rye several
miles inland. Below that ridge now stretches the Romney
Marsh, an area famous for its sheep, who move about as
substitutes for the white fleets of Queen Elizabeth, in a sea of
green instead of a sea of blue.

It is not surprising, therefore, that with all these contriv-
ings to change the spirit of place, the spirit of time should also
have succumbed to the magic. The people in the Marsh are a
leisurely folk, going about their daily lives detached from the
rest of the county, to say nothing of the rest of the world.
Marsh folk have their own traditions and habits. They keep
to themselves. They tend to be elusive. One sees them at a
distance, crossing wide aspects, disappearing into dumpy
cottages, slipping along submerged dykes.

The nearest small town to the Marsh is Appledore. Does
that mean golden apple, or sleeping apple? I am not sure, but
I have my suspicions. They are confirmed by what happened
when I took my French friend to find a cup of tea there after
our archaeological labours at Stone-cum-Ebony. We inquired
at the baker's shop (an Early English building with a shop
ceiling of carved oak timbers), but they could make no tea
there; the fire was out! But we were directed to an inn at the
other end of the village. There we made our way. The door of

the inn was bolted. In front of it stood a small blackboard supported by two bricks. On the blackboard was written in chalk, 'Can you call tomorrow, please, instead of today.' There was no question mark. It was really an order. Whether or not it was directed to seekers after tea, or to some specific body such as the knife-grinder or other local vendor, I shall never know. But I am ready to believe that it was a general statement of the local philosophy in relation to time.

•

OWING TO THE general attitude of mild hostility which our country folk entertain towards all strangers, I had not given much heed to the casual talk about 'the old Swiss watch-maker'. I have lived in our hamlet for ten years, and by now most of its male members have given a hand at some time or other in our garden, and its females have worked in the kitchen. For there is no regular domestic or garden labour here. Everything turns upon the needs of the farmers, who want the women as well as the men for fruit picking, hop 'twiddling' and picking, and 'stringing' in the hop-gardens in spring. So servants come and go, seasonally, and we find our régime is run in a sort of relay system. We are never quite sure who will turn up each morning, for the hamlet arranges the time-table, fitting in our requirements as a secondary source of wage-earning; and strictly secondary. But in this way we have got to know everybody intimately, and they to know us and our momentary doings.

This intimacy has been punctuated with the usual village drama; deaths, marriages, births, and minor scandals. But in the background there has always been this one factor which has never advanced; the presence of the 'Swiss watch-maker', who, we have been told, lives in a cottage which he built forty years ago on a rising bit of ground now entirely hidden by a fir plantation. In that plantation he carries on a small-holding sort of life, even though he is now well over eighty. But we had never seen him, or heard anything definite about him. The references were always casual, as though the matter were of small importance since the old foreigner was not really one of the community. But it was patent that he was accepted, and generally liked in a mild sort of way, so far as our folk can

94

like a stranger who has been living in their midst for only forty years.

I had not even seen the cottage, for the plantation stood between it and the hill road. It was tucked away somewhere behind those dark trees, themselves a foreign element in our land of fruit and chestnut copses. The firs had a sombre, secretive look, as though they too had come from somewhere else. Thus the Swiss watch-maker remained almost legendary; the one element of mystery in a community absolutely English.

One day recently, however, a clock went wrong: an old American pendulum clock, with a picture of the green at Newhaven, Conn. (or is it Penn.?) engraved on its glass door. Why not, I thought, go down and see the Swiss watch-maker about it? So I walked down the hill one Saturday afternoon, found a broken gate fronting the fir copse, and walked up the steep path beneath the trees. The bungalow cottage stood in a clearing at the top: though hardly a clearing, for I presumed that the trees had been planted round the building, originally on open ground. The cottage was L-shaped, and larger than I had expected. Beside it was a second building, long and single-storeyed, with a long workshop window. The way between them was covered in, and I could see through the arch to a yard at the back and a garden beyond, where a fountain and tall grotto stood, covered in weeds. The fountain was asleep, and a gigantic tabby cat was asleep beside it, on the edge of the grotto, which made a sort of miniature Teutonic Venusberg round the tiny pond.

There was neither bell nor knocker, so I rapped with my knuckles at the coloured window-pane of the door. It was blood colour, and through it I could see a curiously tinted interior, as of furniture carved in liver, and visceral curtains. I could see a grandfather clock, sideways on, and it was dressed in the same sanguinary hue. A sound of solemn ticking came through the door. It came through the walls of the cottage too, apparently from every part of the building. Fast and slow, eager and patient, tick-tocking away, the whole house was vibrant with the chorus, as though a host of crickets were chirping on the hearth and under the floors; but crickets of steel, and gut, and brass.

Nobody answered to my knock. I waited as one always waits when calling at a stranger's home. Then I knocked again, and the response startled me; for at least a hundred clocks suddenly chimed the quarter-hour; abrupt, regimented, in a single *alleluia*, then a ringing fall, then silence again, except for the ticking which appeared to have paused for a second, but now went on again. The multitude of voices was disconcerting; high and low, impudent and slow, silver and iron, string and spring, they all leapt out suddenly and were as quickly gone again.

I knocked for the third time, as much out of nervousness as of any real hope of a response from flesh and blood. But this time my rap was answered. I saw a small figure behind the blood curtain of glass. The door opened a few inches, and an elderly lady peered out at me. Her look was mild, as though she did not really expect to see anything tangible, other perhaps than a robin (I was convinced it must be something with a tinge of red). Her surprise, when she saw a human, was registered by an instant change of expression. It gave her genial face a passing gleam of hostility; but that vanished as soon as it appeared, and she looked at me blandly, and waited. I explained my purpose. She nodded, dubiously. 'He's very old,' she said, and she spoke with a rich cockney accent. 'My old cousin's eighty-seven, and he can't see much longer to do fine work. But I'll call him.'

She disappeared, leaving the door open, and I could now see that the narrow hall was not drenched in blood. It was indeed most homely, with the grandfather clock, a heavily carved bench, a still more heavily carved occasional table beyond the bench, and further carved brackets stuck on the walls like swallows' nests, each bearing an elaborate piece of china-ware (Dresden, I presumed). Now that the door was open, the ticking of clocks had swelled to full tide. It surged from every room, like the traffic of horses' hooves on City pavements in the 'nineties.

Then the Swiss watch-maker appeared. His cousin had been to fetch him from the workshop alongside the house. He was wiping his hands on his apron, and I could see his shrivelled and wrinkled face beaming with a smile that made his spectacles ride up and down on his nose. His eyes were bleared with age, but still shone with chips of blue. '*Gum in! Gum in!*' he cried, in a Hansel-and-Gretel voice, as wrinkled as his skin. His German accent was tremendous, as pungent as a piece of Stilton. A long life in England had served only to keep it moist. I won't try to present it phonetically, because the effort would only detract from the dignity of the marvellous old figure whom I want to portray.

I followed him into the room on the right of the passage; and I gasped. It was a large room, but it was filled to capacity with clocks, artificial birds in cages, tables laid with rare pieces of china, paper-weights, old pipes of painted porcelain, ivory fans, and all the rest of the stuff that sentiment and jackdaw habits make us collect. Here was a German interior, from the days of Grimm, and old Sturm of the Confessions, and the Meistersingers. I almost looked round for Papa Haydn!

When I told the old man that it was not a watch but an old German-American clock that was in trouble, he cheered up even more. '*Ach! Mein* eyes are all right for that,' he said. 'I have some nice gut for the lines to the weights; hand-made gut which I have had for sixty years and never used! You bring the clock and I will put him right.'

Already I had my doubts about the Swiss part of the legend. I could recognize something familiar in the build of the man, the structure of the bones in his face, the turn of phrase. I took the plunge. 'Are you from the Schwarzwald?'

I asked abruptly. Perhaps too abruptly, for instantly his face closed; the old eyelids snapped down over those chips of blue. He opened his eyes to look cautiously, almost suspiciously at me. I could see the history of his sojourn in our village written in that glance. Without waiting for him to reply, I asked, 'Do you know the village of Waldkirch, up the little valley of the Elz, near Furtwangen where the museum of clocks is kept?'

The effect of that question was startling. The old cousin, who had been hovering by the door, darted forward and seized me by the hand, tears in her eyes. The old man rose several inches, took off his cap and thrust it into his pocket. Rubbing his head, as though to stir his wits, he cried out in a voice that cracked into falsetto with excitement, '*Do* I know Waldkirch! Why, I *come* from Waldkirch! Now isn't that....' But wonder silenced him. He stared long and earnestly at me, and then shook the hand which his cousin had just relinquished. She meanwhile was making inarticulate noises of incredulity and delight. I had a feeling that she was pressing flagons of lager into my hands, enormous flagons with elaborate, weighted metal lids that shut themselves as soon as the drinker released a thumb from the trigger at the hinge.

The talk now flowed like the Rhine. We recalled people whom we knew in common, the Doctor, the *Oberfurstrat*, the friends who formerly ran the medieval stone-cutting mill (precious stones, cut by peasant women with the aid of water power from the river), the baker who made such wonderful Christmas cakes of hazel-flour and icing. Christmas! It set the old man shaking his head sadly. '*Ach!* I had hoped to go over again one Christmas, to spend it in the old way. But it is gone. That Germany is gone. The blasted Prussians have destroyed it. I left Baden when I was seventeen, for I would *not* serve in the Prussian army, or any army. I went over into Switzerland and learned the watch-making. Then I came to England, and I have not been back. No, never been back.

And now *that* Germany is gone. It was so nice. It was peaceful, that Germany. We loved our life then, in the valleys of the Black Forest, with our costumes and our village bands. And our Christmas times; what times they were, with the snow in the forest, and the walking parties on Christmas morning, up the Kandel, or the Feldberg, and the sun red between the pine trees, and the smell of the fires coming up from the villages.'

The chips of blue in his moist old eyes seemed to grow pale, then to darken as the past gathered in them. He turned helpless to his old cousin, and she looked at him; saw his bereavement, and took his hand. But their sadness did not last. The thrill of meeting somebody who lived so near, and who knew their native place in far-distant Baden, was greater than the burden of recollection and the dying nostalgia for a Grimm's fairyland scene of childhood. The old man cheered up, the chips of blue cleared, the smile once more crossed the old face, and the spectacles bobbed up from his nose.

'You bring the old clock along,' he said. 'I've still got eyesight enough for that!' They both followed me to the door, and again he repeated the injunction to bring the clock along, and the assurance that he could still see that much. I needed no such assurance, however, for I could see those old eyes looking back over three-quarters of a century, to the depths of the Black Forest, with his childhood wandering there fearlessly among the wolves of time, and the hyenas of history.

KENTISH COBS

BETWEEN TWO KENTISH lanes that meet outside my
door, under a canopy of pines and acacias, lies a little spinney
in the form of a triangle, bounded by an apple orchard. Until
this year it has been so dense that even children have not
penetrated there, but last April the farmer (that skilful and
hard-working neighbour of mine whose land-cunning I watch
with constant admiration) has cleaned the spinney, shaping
the trees into a formality that reminded me of stage sets for
some medieval play. The surface of the spinney then revealed
itself as a basin, dropping into the centre where a mass of
primroses and wild hyacinths sprang up, making yet another
theatre set in harmony with the curtain of catkins which
emerged after the pruning. How fresh, innocent and gay was
that scene, with its aureolins, its apple-greens, its girl's-eye
blue. The Angelical Painter of Florence could not have been
more ecstatic.

Now late summer has arrived, and the farmer's main in-

tention shows more clearly. I have never known such a harvest
of nuts. Did I not mention, in my excitement over the colours
and qualities of that small patch of springtime, that the
trees in the spinney were hazels? They now proclaim themselves, for there they stand, their branches decorated with the
gradually grading green of the long filbert nuts starting out of
a coronet of leaves. First they were indistinguishable from the
foliage; but towards the end of July they began to bleach
while the leaves began to darken into the heavy chlorophyll
of autumn. Today, in late August, they hang in shapes like
the languid nails on the hands of some fabulous princess for
whom housework would have been an unknown diversion
detrimental to her beauty. Their colour now is hard to describe. It is not brown. It is not white nor green. Perhaps the
very palest of coffee, flooded in creamy milk, approximates.

In England today, nuts are thought to be a luxury growth,
whose profit has long since been destroyed by the import from
France and Italy. Here and there (as for example round our
county town of Maidstone) one sees the remains of filbert
farms, where the trees are ancient and of gnomic shapes. A
walnut tree, or even a grove here and there, may also be
found; but the harvesting is a private matter, to supply a
country house for Christmas.

Our spinney, this year, has been too lavish in its response
to the pruning to allow of such perfunctory gathering. The
farmer, while inspecting his pampered apple trees, suddenly
caught sight of the cob-nuts, the authentic Kentish cobs. I
was out in my own ground, on the other side of the lane, and
I heard his exclamation. 'Why! Look at those nuts!' he
cried aloud. I think that nobody else was about, and I am
certain that he could not see me, because I was on my knees
weeding a cold-frame full of columbine seedlings. But farmers, like all other solitary workers, have a habit of address-
ing the universe at large, thus peopling their isolation with
a rare fecundity that becomes a society unto itself.

A farmer no sooner sees a crop than he envisages a harvest. Within a day or two, I heard the arrival, at seven one morning, of a van with a load of ladders. Later, after breakfast, half a dozen of the semi-migrant pickers who linger on between the early fruit-picking and the hop-season, came up the hill and went into the spinney. It was still thick enough to swallow them. All I could observe was the swinging of boughs, the occasional emergence of an upright ladder, a head in a cap, an up-stretched arm and hand. All that day the work went on, all the next, and still it continues. And this on a handful of land no bigger than a postage-stamp; or so it must appear even on a large-scale map.

My Corgi has been most agitated by this disturbance so close to his doorstep. It is his daily habit to spend many hours quietly sitting, like one of Landseer's lions, on the grass bank below the elegant yew hedge beside the garage doors. There he rests, with head back, great chest thrust forward, one foot folded against it in a pose reminiscent of the statue of a statesman. Passers-by he will greet with a faint rumble in his throat, or if he recognizes them, with a movement of the stump where other breeds of dog maintain a tail.

With these chattering semi-gypsies about, however, he cannot keep this dignified stance. They shout to each other, crack nuts and throw the shells at him, pass loud remarks about his Welsh characteristics, and even from time to time address my house (though they see nobody about) with calls of 'What's the time, Guvner?' with no respect for person or distinction of class, if there is such a thing in this post-war world.

A gift-basket has been brought by the farmer to our door, and we have been told to keep them towards Christmas, by which time they will have turned to a spaniel-like gold, with a silky surface, and a rich, oily content. There is no flavour quite like them. The walnut is the king of nuts, rich, superb. But these cobs come upon the palate with a delicacy that is foretold in their springtime beginnings, when the trees are princesses in pale silk, with those lovely, languid hands of which I have already spoken. They are to the palate what those primroses were to the eye when my attention was first drawn to the interior of the spinney in April. They are one of nature's extras, to be classed, perhaps, with truffles, or certain green figs eaten warm from the tree, or a greengage that is so full of amber sugars its sides have burst and drops of self-engendered honey coagulated there.

What a county, I say to myself again, that it can be so famous for so many things, and so opulent with memories of history, the comings and goings of the traffic of Europe during two thousand years; yet can have the character to foster an odd variety of nut to which it gives its name, the Kentish Cob, that is sought after all over the gastronomic world; and, on the site of its growth, is a feature of the landscape that adds to the fairy quality of its lanes, giving them a privacy where squirrels lurk, and glow-worms nestle, and schoolboys linger with an estimating eye during the month of July.

To SIGNIFY CONGREGATION, we talk of a brace of partridges, a pride of lions, a school of porpoises, and so on. In the same way I would speak of a miracle of wheat, as the most expressive description of this annual gathering, field by field, of the ears of corn upon which the economy of the human race is established and maintained. For it is a miracle, worldwide and commonplace, like so many of the wonders of the world; a miracle not only of fact, but of symbolism and all the beauty of recollection and association with which the ripening of the corn enriches us year after year.

For over a week, now, I have been disturbed by this spectacle; disturbed, not unhappily, but with an excess of imaginative delight. I can look out of my windows across the valley, and see the same activity as that which is repeatedly pictured in the Bible, and by the makers of the Greek vases and friezes, and by the painters of Europe, yes, and of the Orient too. It is the oldest aspect in our history; for before the sowing of wheat, and the settlements which it necessitated, mankind had no history; only a wandering in the wilderness, a hand-to-mouth existence upon the edge of peril and terror. A handful of wheat, his first reward of constancy to one place and of faith in the future, brought man a symbol of assurance, of long life here and hereafter. It was only after the planting of wheat that longevity and the founding of tradition was established. Man looks across his own harvest fields, and:

'Hence the complexion of his future days.'

I am always filled with astonishment by that sense of recognition with which I gaze at a wheatfield as soon as the ears begin to form. There is something fundamental in that shape; the heavy head, studded with the jewels of grain so closely set that they make a cobbled pattern. It is that pattern which craftsman and artist seized upon at the beginning of civilization, to reproduce in the decoration of houses, weapons, tools, totems, and shrines. It figures in the crowns by which they honour their heroes. That may explain this instant recognition with which individuals, even the most un-historical and ill-educated of us, look upon 'the happy harvest fields'. Racial memory must come into play, a recalling of something that has always been of fundamental importance to our ancestors, and remains so to us, not only as food for our flesh, but also for our faith in Providence. The planting of a field of corn is in itself an act of faith.

So my deep-seated pleasure, as I look out of my window today, a hot August day misty with the promise of long hours of sunshine, is hardly an individual emotion. It is part of my common humanity. Yet it compels me from my personal affairs, and will not be gainsaid. I have to leave the desk and the pen, those symbols of a particular pre-occupation, and I must go out to share in this communal ceremony of the wheatfields.

A farmer over the hill, north of my window and thus beyond my view, has called in the combine harvester this year. It is a novelty in our intimate and comparatively minia-ture countryside, where the fields are of all shapes and sizes, with hedgerows swelling into copses, and patchworks of fruit orchard and hop garden. The combine, that crawling factory, is too massive a mechanism to be used generally amongst us. I have been out, however, to watch it at work down in the Weald, and could well spend a whole day lazily counting the sacks of grain as they fill up on the bridge of the machine, while the bales of tied straw are scratched together and ejected at the back. What a mass of ingenuity! And how much labour and waiting it saves, especially in such a summer as the present one, where the later weeks around the time of

H

ripening, have been sprinkled with showers of rain and sudden thunderstorms, enough to damp the ears and threaten sprouting before they can be threshed. But it is that waiting which is, for our more ritualistic human imagination, the most significant feature of harvesting. The slowness, the patience, the acceptance of unseen forces at work, from the moment of ploughing, through the sowing, the harrowing, the spring growth, the emergence of the ears, the change of colour through several grades of green to a flaxen gold, until the August Age of Bronze, the Roman tinge, that comes with ripeness and the ready moment; all this is part of that accommodation of our human self-discipline to a slow gradualness, by which the architecture of our lives is established on a rock of surety, and not merely on the sands of excitement.

What I missed most, in the fields where the combine was at work, was the period when the wheat rested in stooks. What a shape that is: the waisted tent, yet still of vegetable form, as of a thickset tree! How frequently it figures in the paintings of Brueghel, of Samuel Palmer, of Turner and Constable, and in the little woodcuts of Bewick, that divine illustrator whose tiny colophons are in their perfect way a story of England. I have been thankful again this year that the fields within my range of vision, from this window, have been mowed by the more familiar cutter-and-binder. One year, after disastrous winds had flattened the war-time corn (before the newly ploughed pastures were firm enough to contain the tall crops) the two sloping fields, open to the southwest gales, had to be cut by hand. That was a spectacle I shall remember for ever. It was the Bible story, and the classics of Greece and Rome, all contained in a single scene. Four men began by going round the headland, some ten feet out from the hedges, with sickles. Next day they began with scythes, standing in a line, and swinging their blades together, like a flight of planes curving in formation through the sky. I listened, hour by hour, to the song of the scythe-steel ringing against the resisting stalks of the near-infinity of wheat. How many thousands of years had that shrill whine been known to human ears? It came to mine and carried me back through time to the beginning of things, the Golden Age, the birth of art, crafts and science, of human society itself. No historian had ever touched me so instantly to panoramic vision along the centuries.

The sight of the great campus of stooks, mounds of gold upon a golden field, has the same effect upon me. I am standing now, as I dictate these words, looking out at this besieging army tented through the valley, and once more I marvel at the wealth of which we all are capable, given the industry and the faith in the future. In these time-honoured forms, standing securely, awaiting the threshing, is a currency that will never fluctuate. Here is the bread of man: and in that word bread, as we all know, there is the realization not only of food, but of a sacrament.

ONE OF THE most remarkable features of our local country-side is, or hitherto has been, the lack of sparrows. Our Kentish copses, and our abundance of tall and deep hedges, and also our orchards of cherry, apple and plum, are all attractive to bird life, and the devoted watcher can find this part of England to be a paradise of his particular delights. Every kind of finch abounds, as also those rogues the blue tits. The general, predominant, bird-in-the-street is the chaffinch, with his gregariousness and his variety of songs. We know him by his rusty poll and his patch of white. The robin, of course, is always about, bold and upright, with a stance that always reminds me of the speaking figure of the late David Lloyd-George; legs slightly unsteady and concave, chest thrown out, and head cheekily perked up in defiance. 'That little hunchback in the snow,' he has been called by the poet W. H. Davies. And so he is in the cold weather, for nothing stops his foraging. But he is always bold, and will come to sit on the handle of my spade when I stop digging, to mop my steaming head.

The jay and the magpie, exotic creatures in our northern climate of temperate habits, are always to be seen, the jay rushing neurotically from tree to tree, *skwarking* as he goes; the magpie dragging his heavy tail across the sky as though the weight is almost too much for him to remain airborne, his progress being a series of rear falls and recoveries. Both birds are vagabonds, and the farmers are not too kind to them. They rob the orchard and vegetable garden. But even so, I find it difficult to make war upon them, for their beauty is great, and there are not so many of them, even in these post-war days when the farmers are too busy to spend their time out with a gun.

Blackcaps, bullfinches, and even the rare goldfinch are regular in their attendance upon the enticements offered on my top terrace; scraps of fat from the kitchen, overdone pieces of toast, meaty bones which the Corgi has been too lazy to bury for his future use. Wagtails and the yaffle pay a visit occasionally, the latter flashing away like a tropical vision, with a derisive guffaw, even if some human indoors merely approaches a window to admire him.

For years this patronage of our bird table and the top lawns has gone on. But not until last summer did I see a sign of the common sparrow, that *gamin* of the bird world. And when he did come, how unlike the London sparrow he was. His feathers were rich, fawn and umber, and he was sleek and graceful in build; unlike the sooty town bird. I admired him as something rare, and decided that he must be a tree sparrow. I noticed how shy he was, hovering in the background amongst the crowding tits and finches. One or two starlings alighted, strutting about like policemen, and the sparrow flew off to a red-plum tree, his sombre colours lost among the liver-tinted leaves.

Next day he came again, and hopped about the lawn on the outskirts of the crowd. This time he picked up a crumb or two from their rich table, darting in where a greedy blue tit or even a ring-dove had dropped more than they could carry. It was a pretty sight, the modesty of the creature. His whole attitude was an apology for the intrusion. Where had he come from? That I shall never know. But two days later he came with a mate, an even rustier little object. She did not dare to forage, but stood still while the male performed his Lazarus act once more.

The pair lingered in the neighbourhood of the garden all through the autumn. Towards winter they were joined by a second pair. We had four sparrows, who seemed in the mood for squatting. The migrants departed, and this loss emphasized the presence of the brown-coats, and the chirpings that now could be heard after daybreak and continuously through the hours of sunshine—and of rain too, for it became a feature of our country life, this *cheep-cheep*, so monotonous yet so cheery, maintained even when the days were dreary with leaden skies and the steady drip of rain. The sparrows appeared to have a faculty for finding shelter, and somewhere about the walls of the house, for I could hear them constantly now, while sitting at work; *cheep-cheep*, the voice of anonymity, the humble and ever-present.

Ever-present! Yes, that was the potent factor. Those four sparrows were joined by another pair before Christmas, and when the snowy weather of January drove the blue tits and the great tits to a congregation about our bird table, we found that already there was a rival party to dispute the distribution and the economic law.

Then came spring, and the six sparrows, augmented by some relatives introduced clandestinely, I know not when, began an activity almost ominous in its resolute co-ordination. Everything was so patently worked out beforehand. Those eight—no, sixteen—sparrows lost no time or energy in wasteful movement. They knew exactly where to find the bits and pieces (most of the stuff rejected by the more spectacular and prouder tits), and what to do with them. The chosen spots for building, skilfully pre-selected, rapidly became adapted to the requirements of the intruders. Under every gutter and in every roof gulley, the scuffle of claws, the scraping of wings, the angry *cheep-cheep* of harassed workers, went on from morning until night. And soon the colony was complete, and a huge traffic of supply was organized by the males. Voices multiplied as the spring days lengthened. I had no peace now, because of the parliament that never ceased around my study windows.

Now it is summer, and the new generation of sparrows is abroad, as active and as big as its elders. And it has multiplied a hundredfold, its members dominating the meetings on the terrace and round the bird table. Further, its activities have spread to the kitchen garden, and peas are being filched, soft fruits stolen, even the seed beds of lettuce and spinach ravished and reduced to a dust-bath. I am told that I must get some cartridges and bring out the family shot-gun which last saw daylight during the days of the Home Guard in war time. I agree. Self-preservation, to say nothing of the rights of the blue tit, robin, and the singing thrushes, must be considered.

Yet this morning, after a night of rain, I went out in the steamy sunshine, and saw a sparrow alight on a spray of water-jewelled foliage in a greengage tree. He shook the twig, and the drops flew around him, opals of light. He danced on the twig, shook out some more raindrops, and actually chased them in the air, with open beak! Could any man bring a gun to that scene?

THE LAND OF THE DARK TOWER

WHEN I WAS a child of seven, I read a story in the *Boy's Own Paper* called 'The Last of the Paladins', and I believe it was there that I first met the name Rocamadour. For fifty years it has lodged in my memory, and imagination has worked upon it as an oyster works upon a grain of sand to make a pearl. It was not long after this first contact that I came upon those three mysterious lines sung by Edgar in *King Lear*:

> 'Childe Rowland to the dark Tower came;
> His word was still "Fie, foh and fum,
> I smell the blood of a British man".'

This was followed some ten years later by reading Browning's poem based on the first of those three lines of Shakespeare. It was a haunting piece, set in the picture of a countryside forbidding, yet attractive, some half-deserted, upland country

112

of stunted oak forests and ranges of hills, broken by chasms, within whose dark ravines troubled rivers murmured and fretted.

All this was merely literary experience, but it matured in my mind and became a reality, part of that self which lies in the depths of us all, sooner or later to command us towards some fruitful action.

I have just had occasion to obey that command. I have visited Rocamadour and put a fantasy of fifty years to the test of actuality. How seldom it is that the dream is surpassed by the event; but more than once during my visit and wanderings in that unfrequented part of France, the expectation has been quite inadequate when brought into contact with reality. As well as going to Rocamadour, I visited also the underground river at Padirac, nearby, and I made the fifty-mile journey northward to explore the caves at Lascaux, where prehistoric paintings were discovered by some schoolboys in 1940.

These three experiences were highlights during a fortnight's touring in the Department of le Lot, the upland country, lying roughly due east of Bordeaux and west of the Massif Centrale. The month was May; the small strips of rocky land, some of which were still being ploughed by oxen yoked in the Old Testament manner, were knee-high with corn or rich, silky rye grass. Over this undulating country, a thousand feet above sea level, ran what is known locally as the *Causse*. This consists of stunted forest, mainly oak and walnut, heavily draped in grey fungi, broken by a lavish outcropping of limestone rock and shale. In the patches of open country this becomes a kind of grotto-land, where every kind of miniature flora is to be found, and the great swallow-tail butterflies too. The soil among this volcanic debris is of the colour of freshly roasted and ground coffee. The plough turns it to bronze, and it shines in the sun with such a metallic fierceness that it can be seen through the crops and the grass, like the sunburnt scalp of an old peasant through his wisps of grey hair.

This grotto-land is punctuated with juniper bushes and twisted hawthorns, wayfaring tree and bramble. In every bush a nightingale was shouting. We could see the little songsters as we walked past their rostrums. Their small, fawn-feathered bodies throbbed with the violence of their music, which poured out mechanically over a lower beak opening and shutting as though on a hinge. Sometimes in a dip of ground we saw a lake of narcissus flowers, stretching like a neglected pocket of frost. Among the dry rocks the harebells, the camomile, the hellebore, the rock-rose made a paradise where lizards flickered to and fro and fritillaries hovered. Standing up amongst these frailer beauties were small forests of orchids, purple, white, dun-coloured.

Open country indeed! The sense of being up, in the wide air on top of the world, was in itself an adventure. Fold upon fold the forest and the wide scrub-land stretched into the blue distance for fifty miles, scored by a lacy network of dry-walling, with here and there decorative knots of faded red and cream. These knots were villages, hamlets, sometimes a solitary *château* perched impossibly on the edge of a cliff, or what one would expect to be a waterless hill top. There was nothing new amongst these human habitations. The countryside might have been arrested in its development sometime about the middle of the seventeenth century.

Outstanding amongst these knots in the lace of French civilization is Rocamadour, the fabulous village whose name has tolled like a bell in the tower of my imagination for half a century. It clings like a cluster of swifts' nests on the side of one of these inland cliffs, of which I have already spoken. The whole of the Department is really a honeycomb, a kind of brittle and aerated crust riddled with caverns and grottoes scored by innumerable chasms, some of them several miles in extent and hundreds of feet in depth. Nature has draped them with hanging woods and all manner of creeping plants, which quilt the savagery and the abruptness of these volcanic breaks. But this gentleness of time does not hide from the human eye the evidence of past cataclysms and internal upheavals too horrible to imagine. Even this frozen survival of such a past period in the geological story of the earth is sufficient to dwarf, not only the history of man, but that of all organic life. Behind this undulating countryside of flowers, butterflies, enchanted nightingales, rose-coloured villages and all the moss-clad evidence of France's continuous history, there lurks this reminder of the rocks, this warning of what has been. And yet it is here, in this region of a thinly veiled threat, that mankind has probably been settled from the very beginning when *homo sapiens* first emerged from his war with the giants, only to be confronted with the problems of how to survive during the last glacial age. It may have been that during the descent of the Polar ice, northern mankind found its only shelter in those regions where some form of subterranean life was possible. The thousands of caves and grottoes in this part of France offered that shelter, and evidence of it is emerging from time to time in the discoveries of the rock paintings, made not less than thirty thousand years ago.

These records are alike in their hints about the conditions under which life was maintained during that last period of excess in the drama of earth's story. The pictures in the caves at Lascaux, the latest to be discovered, have already been largely written about and photographed. The *Mercure de France* has published a descriptive volume full of beautifully coloured plates, and in England Faber & Faber has published a similar volume. But the most faithful reproduction of these animal drawings, the reindeer, the mammoths, the bison, the attenuated bipeds with bird-like heads, fails to transport the awe-inspiring effect of the whole when seen in the caves. What impressed me was the fact that many of the white limestone surfaces were palimpsests, which had been scored over with figures laid upon each other, some of them upside down, during long periods of time. The later paintings were heavier in drawing and colour than those beneath them, and probably the evolution of style, and in some instances the decadence, must represent many centuries during which the caves were used for ritualistic purposes.

The symbolism, in all its amazing economy and its gradual changes, remains to be interpreted. Contained in it is the story of those tens of thousands of years which must have passed, during which generations of the timid race of man maintained a conservative existence, under a monotony of fear and doggedness, with no significant change in the minds of individuals or in the structure of society. The dominant note of consciousness amongst those primitive men must have been the conviction that there they were, and there they would remain until the end of time in that same condition. It is only during the last two thousand years or so that they have been proved to be wrong. But that may be a bold statement. Our recent history, from the making of the Pyramids onwards to the making of the Atom Bomb may be a mere flash of wayward activity, after which we shall return to the caves.

The second thing that impressed me about the paintings at Lascaux was their appearance of freshness. In one of the smaller tunnels leading out from the left of the larger cave where the accidental entrance was made by the schoolboys (now secured from draughts by iron doors) the limestone walls stretch for some yards with a surface of the most delicate cream colour. The paintings on this surface are so sensitive and so sophisticated in their elimination of unnecessary lines, that I had the impression of being in a fashionable Parisian café, decorated by artists as a means of paying their bills. The freshness was due to the fact, as throughout the rest of the cave, that nature had coated the whole surface with a transparent mineral layer of crystalline purity. In addition to the large paintings, I found on close examination that the whole surface of the walls of the cave was etched with thumb-nail drawings, usually of the heads of the reindeer and the bison. Was this perhaps the first evidence of a system of banking? But this is a dangerous theme to speculate on vaguely, and it is better left to the archaeologists.

But to return to Rocamadour and more recent legend and history! I made my headquarters some four miles away in a picturesque old *château*, now being run as a most comfortable hotel. It is called the Château de Roumégouse, and stands in a handsome park on a hill top, overlooking a fertile valley and the small town of Gramat. From its terrace can be seen the topmost of the series of shrines at Rocamadour. The rest are on the sides of the precipice below. Between the *château* and the fabulous village, there is another of these volcanic ravines, at the bottom of which stands the ruin of an ancient water-mill built in the Roman fashion. The road stretches on between walnut trees until it reaches the edge of the gorge of the Alzou, one of the many tributaries of the Dordogne, that glorious river which flows right through the Department toward the Gironde, and the land of the most famous vineyards of Bordeaux. The vines are gradually returning to the Dordogne district after the disastrous attacks in the past of the phylloxera.

This gorge of the Alzou is characteristic of the many which wrinkle the face of the Department. Both sides are steep, in some places precipitous, with the rock strata exposed in long horizontal designs. These formations have been weathered by time and the hand of man. The village stands prominently where the gorge curves and thus forms a cap round the bend of the cliff. The road to Cahors lies at the bottom and the buildings begin abruptly, rising up the steep so that the foundation of one house is at the roof level of another. Dominating the whole are the *château* and the several shrines. Legend says that the saint, known as Amadour, was the publican, Zaccheus, who climbed the sycamore tree the better to see Our Lord. After the Crucifixion he came to Gaul with his wife, Veronica, and following her death, he founded an Oratory in honour of the Virgin Mary on this spot. It is certain that, in the eighth century, the great Charlemagne passed through here on his return from Lombardy, attended by his nephew, that romantic paladin, Roland. The shrine must have been already famous because Roland left his battle-scarred sword before the altar as an act of worship and thanksgiving. Was this place then the 'dark Tower' pictured by the mad Edgar, and seized upon by Robert Browning as a symbol on which to hang one of his psychological and poetic inquiries into the nature of human motives? I like to think it may be, for the name of the village has that ring about it, the deep and solemn bell-sound. Rocamadour!

No! The magic has not departed from that incantation which has haunted my mind for fifty years, though I have now brought the whole fantasy down to earth. History bears me out, for this inaccessible village, far from main roads and any large town, was the first place of pilgrimage in Christianized France. In the most holy of the chapels stuck on the cliff, there is a wooden Madonna and Child, only fifteen inches in length. It was carved in the eighth century and is blackened with smoke from votive candles offered before it during twelve hundred years. The figure has a narrow cast, the arms close into the sides and the Child a continuation of the shin-bone. It is thus hardly more than a pillar, and the head of the Virgin has an oriental impassiveness and inscrutability. It is so early that its Christian identity has hardly emerged from the anterior religions of the Orient. The features might be those of an epicene Buddha, or of the Egyptian Osiris. It is an image that represents the parting of the ways, and this way is into Europe. Upon those smoke-darkened lineaments, and in those closely clasped arms, there lies the seed of the Gothic cathedrals, and the emphasis upon individual idiosyncrasy.

The annual pilgrimage from all parts of Europe has gone on ever since and continues even today. Every year in September the devout people come and climb some two hundred stone steps from the lower to the upper shrines, on their knees, praying as they mount. This festival was interrupted by the Hundred Years War. It has to be remembered that the whole countryside (for this was part of Aquitaine) was dominated by the English. To this day the scars remain in the memories of the peasants. One night, at dinner, I told the old servant at the Château, that we had walked that day through a village called Thégra, where a half-ruined *château* stood in the midst of some medieval dwellings, the shadow of its tower lying across the tiny market-place. 'Yes,' said the servant, 'the English did that. It is not wise to let them know there that you are English!' She was referring to the wars of Edward III, and I began to imagine that I had received some black looks while sightseeing in Thégra.

I still have not begun to describe my coming to Rocamadour, or even to make clear to myself the difference, or maybe the identity, between the fifty-year-old dream and the village of stone and sunshine in that urgent country where nature still has something of terror close beneath the surface. But is not that too a characteristic of the world of dream?

MEASURELESS CAVERNS

ALL MY LIFE I have been hypnotized by those wonderful lines in Coleridge's poem *Kubla Khan*:

> 'Where Alph the sacred river ran
> Through caverns measureless to Man.'

I never thought that one day I should see with my own eyes a reality which should put upon me a spell of enchantment even greater than that conjured by these lines through my imagination during the past half century. But it has been so. I had occasion recently to go to Paris to lecture, and after my duties were completed, I found myself moved by an irresistible impulse to go southward. Paris in May-time, with the chestnut avenues in the Luxembourg Gardens flaunting their creamy candles, the traffic up and down the Champs-Élysées glittering in the sun, the sense of hope and renewed vitality throughout the Queen of Cities, all these things set me longing for a further adventure before returning to 'the daily round, the common task'.

So my not-unwilling companion and I took a train one morning from the Austerlitz Station. It was a spotlessly clean train, and we had a well-cooked luncheon during the journey; unaccustomed novelties for English people. We crossed the Loire at Orléans, and saw the cathedral standing up over the town, honey-coloured in the sunshine. The flat country cultivated in strips of corn gave place to more interesting downland with woodland valleys and little streams flowing southward. The undulations increased, the valleys became richer, the streams more turbulent, until at last on our right hand there flowed and bubbled the beautiful Coreze. It was a living creature running by our side, dropping over falls and rushing through fringes of wild iris. In the distance, on our left, were the dim shapes of the Massif Centrale, the most wild and unfrequented part of France. In mid-afternoon we reached the little town of Brive, where we changed into a local train with wooden seats. Here we sat amongst the peasants and shared the conversation about local scenes and events, all of primary importance. After an hour of this hot and animated intercourse we got out at Roc Amadour, where we found waiting for us a specially chartered little motor-bus, whose outlying parts were tied up with pieces of rope. Twenty minutes' run in this hazardous conveyance brought us to the *château* where we were to stay for a few days.

It was a fabulous, rather than a real, place, though built massively enough of the local stone, with two great towers and terraces upheld by bastions, overgrown with every conceivable kind of rock plant, amongst which the lizards darted with little rustling sounds, more quiet than silence itself.

What a hospitable reception we had from our host and hostess in this remote place. Taking tea on the terrace, with a view before us stretching for fifty miles, a little thunderstorm

I

in the distance passing over the scene as a complete object in itself, as though represented by Albrecht Dürer; solidity of clouds in an otherwise clear sky, a livid under-side flushed with occasional gleams of lightning, a distant rumble, and a few vertical rods to indicate rain. In the valley below us lay a medieval village called Rignac, with its rose-coloured roofs outlined in ivory, and another *château* dominating it. Below us, in every bush, the nightingales poured out their throbbing music, never ceasing; drumming on our ears with their ancient story:

> 'Perhaps the self-same song that found a path
> Through the sad heart of Ruth, when, sick for home,
> She stood in tears amid the alien corn;
>   The same that oft-times hath
> Charm'd magic casements, opening on the foam
> Of perilous seas, in faery lands forlorn.'

Above this mad and impulsive music there hovered a shrill overtone, the chirping of myriads of crickets, the smaller brothers of the cicada. It was almost a visible sound, like a silver glaze on the trembling surface of the hay fields. We were already in the magic land of Theocritus and Claude Lorraine, where every tree was doubled in its riches by its own shadow, and all the water sang.

It was not long before we were sufficiently recovered from our journey to begin to look for closer contact with the countryside. We set out for a walk beyond the gates of the park. Leaving its noble timber, we found ourselves on the upland *Causse*, as the whole of this countryside is called by the French. It consists of stunted oak forest, with patches of walnut and small bush; dog-rose, juniper and other fragrant shrubs. The soil is poor, cropping out in coffee-coloured patches between the massive rock and shale, so meagrely that it has to be cultivated with ploughs pulled by oxen, harnessed in exactly the same way as we see them yoked in pastoral scenes on Greek vases spun two thousand years ago.

The nightingales flitted along beside us as we followed one of the network of stony footpaths lined with dry wall. Above us two buzzards wheeled lazily. Swifts cut the air around us, their wings hissing with speed. So it went on, a kind of entranced monotony, fold merging into fold of this rich, yet arid, landscape, with breaks from time to time into abrupt chasms to remind us of a volcanic past.

It is of that past and its tremendous creations, its gigantic sculpturings and its Dantesque achievements, that I intended to write here, as manifested in the world-famous underground river at Padirac. But that is too vast a subject for me to handle so casually at the end of my introduction, so I will return to it later, and try in vain to show how for once, expectation will be exceeded by realization.

OF ALL THE volcanic marvels in the district of the Dordogne in South-Central France, the Gouffe de Padirac is the most impressive. That is how I should open a description of this place if I were writing a guide-book. But I am trying to do something more elusive; I am trying to capture the spirit of the place, to evoke the thousand details of earth, air and water which move together to make one of nature's symphonic masterpieces. I say symphonic, because my first abiding impression is one of sounds, and cessations from sound. We came over the sun-drenched scrub through a running commentary of nightingales, with an occasional diapason of sheep bells, deep-throated cluckings rather than bell tones, flat notes that by contrast emphasized the full and penetrating rapture that poured from the throats of the nightingales.

It was the sudden stopping of this music that made us aware of a change in the landscape. Around us the scrub-land still stretched in all directions over the folding hills. We walked on another fifty yards and saw before us what must have been the cause of the silence. We were silent too. The sight was awe-inspiring. Abruptly, and unperceived until we had mounted the gradual rise, the surface of the earth was broken. We stood on the edge of a vast pit, or well, some hundred yards in diameter. The sides fell vertically and for the first hundred feet were draped with vegetation, small bushes of elder and broom, patches of foxglove, figwort and columbine. A handrail had been put up round the precipice. We peered over it into the dusk and could see, some five hundred feet below, a hillock of rubble scored with mosses and patches of damp. We could hear a trickle of water, but saw none. A few sand-martins were planing tirelessly, making figures of eight among the cool airs of the well, and disturbing the gradual movement upward of a thin mist that rose from the bottom. We could feel its wintry fingers on our skin.

An elaborate structure of iron-work had been erected to support an electric lift, and we took this help which landed us almost at the bottom of the gigantic well. We were still in the open air, though above us the sides of the well, massive groins of rock, appeared to be closing in at the top where the green foliage glittered in what seemed to be artificial sunlight.

We looked around us, first wiping the mist from our spectacles. Staircases of concrete and rock, greasy with a small moss, led downward towards a hole at the bottom of the well. We began to descend, clutching a clammy iron rail somewhat apprehensively. Winding our way downward, we saw where a head of water had bored its way through the hillock of rubble, which now formed the floor of the well. We could hear the water forcing its way. We could hear also the slow drip of water filtering through the fissures of rock and dropping with a clock-like regularity, making a curtain of beads in front of the hole which the staircase now invited us to enter. We put on our raincoats, took a deep breath and passed through the curtain. Here began another world.

The steps still went down. They might have gone down into infinity, for at first we could see only a few yards in the light offered by electric lamps cunningly concealed. But our eyes became accommodated to the loss of daylight, and revealed to us a tunnel dropping irregularly with great striations of rock that made us feel giddy. The staircase made by human hands crept humbly down the decline. At the bottom of this dreadful slope we came to the river. Here it was about twelve feet wide. Its surface made a perfect mirror, for its flow was undisturbed. It moved almost in silence. An occasional whisper, an occasional cluck, as drops from the roof of the tunnel fell on to that mirror and seemed to break into pieces on the hard surface of the water, to be scattered over it. There was no sign of life; not a bud, not a blade: only by the electric lamps a little breath of moss, a dim stirring of life toward this apprehension of light.

We followed our guide along a ridge beside the water, still moving downwards, unless this was an illusion due to the gradual expansion of the sides and top of the tunnel. So we went on expectantly, every electric lamp an adventurous period of our exploration. We could now see more distinctly, and could marvel at the spectacle steadily unfolding itself like the smoky billows of some vast conflagration. The rocky sides rolled down from the darkness above us, arrested torrents of stone, in every liquid shape that the imagination could conceive; but that flood had been fixed into a massive immobility myriads of eons ago. There they were, however, flood upon flood of stony billows pouring down, timelessly rigid, yet here and there seeming to move still in the deception of trickling waters shifting like living skin over them. It was this gentle surface caress, continued through millions of years, which had put upon the naked limestone a veneer of colours and shapes as subtle and fantastic as the ornaments in an oriental temple. The colours were sombre, moving through a dusty spectrum, but they were suitable to our expectation of the landscape of an underworld.

I cannot say after a time, for we had left time itself beyond that curtain of water-drops at the entrance to the tunnel. I must substitute by saying after a space (but space also is of a dubious dimension). We came, let me say, timeless and spaceless, to a sudden end of the ledge where we had accompanied the river. The water widened out, filling the whole floor of the tunnel, and the tunnel spread its sides and roof to the dimensions of a cathedral. We embarked on a punt and the guide stood at the back paddling the craft along. This change of motion made the silence even more impressive. There was no longer the sound of our own footfalls; we could hear only the whisper of the stream, the gurgle of the paddle, the metronomic drip out of the darkness above us. One by one the little electric oases of light, each with its touch of moss, guided us down this dream river. The fantasy grew, it swelled like a great burst of music, for the tunnel now was no longer a tunnel, the river was no longer a river. We floated across a lake, which made a glassy floor, to a vast cavern soaring up for thirteen hundred feet, supported by great columns and pillars carved, with the chemistry of time, into shapes wilder than any chiselled by Gothic craftsmen. Lights had been fixed high up, revealing the whole splendour. There we sat on the surface of the water, caught up into the pattern because the reflection below us was as rigid and as perfect as the dreadful stability above. Thus we hovered like ephemerids in the midst, a tiny continent of wonder and worship. There my memory will remain, while life lasts.

No matter how old we may be in heart and mind, with consequent dullness of response to things and events in the world around us, there are certain experiences which penetrate the most heavily calloused temperament, to touch the spirit with the prickings of youth. As we grow older, we learn to become more and more grateful for these small, stabbing experiences, these casual moments when we are surprised by what the poet Keats called 'a fine excess'. But it need not be even an excess. The revelations of joy and wonder can come, as they came to William Blake, through a grain of sand held in the hand, or the angelic flash of sunlight illuminating the flowering bush in a suburban lane.

I find myself already prepared to contradict myself, for after all, it is not so infrequently that these inspiring moments come in the autumn of life. Scarcely a day passes between dawn and sunset without some unseen remembrancer jogging the elbow of my attention to point out a miniature drama in which perfection triumphs over the ordinary and the habitual. I can look back, for example, over the past few hours as I sit here on a cold spring night, half asleep and bemused under the kindness of a fire of pear logs. I have just looked out of the terrace door to let the dog in, and I felt the frost settling over a windless world. The footpath of the Milky Way was thick with star dust. Betelgeuse and Rigel flamed in the south, with Sirius chasing them. The hard light of the stars, and the bite of the air drove me back to the fireside, and there I have been sitting among the cushions of reminiscence, contrasting the icy aspect of the night sky, in its deadly silences, with the springtime world through which my dog and I wandered only this afternoon.

The day had begun with frost and mist, through which the sun rose blood-red and flattened behind the silhouette of a ridge of naked trees. He soon gained power, and by the time he had reached his zenith, the frost was sublimed, disappearing in ethereal whiffs above the grass and out of the branches of tree and bush. Walking in the early afternoon round the northern foot of a wooded hill, I found that still there were several pockets where the frost lurked. Catkins hung disconsolately over the grey carpet, and I passed these pallid areas with a catch in my breath, as the cold air from them entered my lungs.

All this took place in an almost unnatural stillness and quietude. Not a bird sang, and my urchin Corgi found nothing to excite his nose at burrow mouth or along the frozen runnels. It was not until the lane brought us up the hill and through a hanging wood to the top that we entered one of those fields of revelation of which I have spoken. The Corgi was the first to respond to the sun-change of circumstances. Up went his ears, and with an audible twitching of nostrils, he was off on the heels of a scent. Then I too awoke from my low-temperature lethargy. Emerging from the wood I looked up at the last of its tall trees to see a host of rooks at work, a garrulous committee boisterously concerned with house repairing and the signing of leases. The croaks and cries of their legal proceedings were deafening, and I felt that a philosopher could have made capital by contrasting the din and anxiety of these black-coated citizens with the almost mystical silence of their shadows flitting to and fro on the sun-bright surface of the lane which was now warm to my feet.

I walked on, my senses expanding like an opening flower as I advanced into the open south, where all the promise of coming spring lay before me. Gradually leaving the clamorous rooks, I turned over the brow of the hill and there took the full embrace of the sun. A spectrum shook before my eyes. My skin tingled with life, radio-active life whose vitality was almost alarming. Then suddenly the revelation came. I realized that the torpor of time was broken. Here, on the sloping lands toward the gravid year, life already was beginning its recurrent miracles. I heard the trickle of water in the ditch beside the lane, and this sound was quickly augmented by the rustle of leaves, as a field-mouse took precautionary measures before the clumsy approach of my Corgi, who by now was almost frantic with the press of his engagements. Then a robin became importunate, flitting along beside me like a Neapolitan boy offering to show me the sights. He chattered away above his little buff waistcoat, making a good pretence of introducing me to the festivity which I now beheld.

The tribulet opened into a wayside pool over which hung a willow. It was here that I stopped, listened, then looked. A vague commotion of sound centralized itself and fixed my attention with it. I recognized the rich communion of wings, an Aeolian music comprised of the willing conflict between gauze and air. A host of bees was out, and at work, hovering and alighting, and hovering again, repeating the process in their thousands, gathering the first golden pollen of the year from the trembling blossoms of the pussy-willow. My eyes were confused between the myriad furry bodies and furry blooms. All alike were in commotion, giving and taking these first pure prospects, which I knew through my faith to be the sign of the year's redemption.

AN OLD-ENGLISH FOREST

IF I WERE given leisure enough, I should like to follow
one of my numerous creative desires, and give myself during
a complete cycle of the four seasons, to wandering about
England collecting material for a history of the English
forests. What a vast ambition! I should need to be as deep-
natured as Shakespeare, Spenser and Wordsworth, the three
poets who immediately occur to my imagination as masters of
the tree-lore peculiar to our mossy island, where the arboreal
growth is as distinctive and idiosyncratic as that of our individual men and women down the ages.

The history of our woods is closely bound with that of our
splendours and our economics, the two extremes which in
emulsion make the somewhat cloudy mixture known as our
national story. Most of our forests have been royal preserves,
hunting grounds where our kings have disported themselves
with the gay company of their courts. So in that aspect my
book would be full of the pageantry and the majesty which
are so rapidly disappearing from human society today.
Imagine the record of costumes and customs, the pictures of
fair ladies and their dandified knights with all the trimmings
and the paraphernalia of chivalry during its hours of

recreation in the sylvan hunt. The colours and the gestures dazzle my eyes.

On the other hand, the enclosure, preservation, and up-keep of our royal forests have played an expensive part, and this would have to be duly recorded in the ledgers of the centuries. For several hundred years after the coming of the Normans in the eleventh century, vast tracts of the country, such as the New Forest in Hampshire, the Forest of Anderida which ran for one hundred and forty miles through the Weald of Kent, Surrey and Sussex into Hampshire, and Epping Forest in Essex, were kept intact only at the expense of the people. Many of their ancestors of purely Anglo-Saxon blood were expropriated from their freeholds in and on the edges of these great hunting preserves, with the result that agricultural development, and the necessary growth of popu-lation, were to that extent arrested. But I do not want to get diverted into pounds, shillings and pence, for in this modern world there is already too much emphasis upon the economic side of life and the part it is alleged to play in our personal destinies. I prefer for a moment at least to escape from such considerations and to wander in the woods, looking for the monarchs of the past, some of whose sentinels remain as oak, cedar, yew to make a kind of ghostly Witanagemot, a council of elders whose foliage still whispers of a vanished legislature.

Most of the great forest of the Weald has disappeared, consumed as charcoal for the smelting of the iron-ore in the soil beneath it. Much of the New Forest remains, and by a happy chance of municipal legislation, Epping Forest on the north-eastern outskirts of London, will survive for all time as a national park.

I have just been looking through the text and the hundreds of superb photographs of a book called *London's Epping Forest* (Country Life Ltd., 30*s*.) written by James A. Brimble. The photographs alone are an enchantment for they show every aspect of the Forest, at all times of day and night, and in the

dress of all four seasons. We see solitary giants standing deep
in snow across which beams from a horizontal winter sun
throw an illusion of quilting. We see swampy clearings
where water plants cluster round the roots of alders which
lean over a brackish floor where wild lilies are rising from the
ooze. There are heathery tracks across patches of open
country which I know from experience must be busy with the
turmoil of armies of giant ants, moving amid the fragrance
from the heather bells and all other perfumes of the rabbit-
cropped heath, where the blossom is all in miniature.

It is incredible to believe that this remote and timeless
scene is within half an hour's journey of the Bank of England.
Again and again an odd corner or a wide panorama offers
itself to be instantly recognized as a picture that might have
been painted by Constable, Peter de Wynt or John Crome.
Here is England as it was in the time when King Oberon of
the fairies quarrelled with his queen, Titania, and greeted her
in the woods with the angry but beautiful pentameter:

'Ill-met by moonlight, proud Titania!'

Once I possessed a fifteenth-century dower house in East
Anglia, formerly belonging to the Earls of Worcester, and it
was my habit to drive down as often as possible for a period of
solitude in this ancient building made of old ships' timbers
and wattle and daub. That drive took me through the whole
length of Epping Forest, sometimes at midnight, and I recall
many an experience of wonder when I stopped to make
obeisance at the rising of the moon, or before the entangle-
ment of glittering planets and constellations amongst the
branches of some misshapen old giant planted perhaps by one
of Queen Elizabeth's foresters to replace timber taken for the
building of the little ships which were to fight against the
Spanish Armada.

Now that we are at peace again I intend to go back to

explore farther into Epping Forest, and I shall do so with greater understanding through having accompanied Mr Brimble as historian, gamekeeper, naturalist and attractive companion, whom I shall expect at any moment to introduce me to Rosalind and Celia, and Jaques, the philosopher beneath the trees.

WIND AND WATER

AFTER THREE YEARS of near-drought, with ponds looking like dirty saucers, brooks a mere dribble, ditches stony gullies where the rabbits sit to dream of succulence while nibbling at the withered grasses, suddenly wind and rain have come. And they have come in abundance, like boys bursting out of school. For over two weeks now the house has rocked and swayed under the assault, and the cone-aerial outside my window has been playing Aeolian tunes night and day, to the detriment of both sleep and work.

The tune is only one of the orchestral effects of this late-winter romp of the elements. It puts in the piccolo parts, shrill and limited to a range of about four tones, sliding up and down between them until I am tempted to open the window and to wrench the involuntary musical instrument from the wall. But were I to open the window I cannot imagine what would happen; for it looks out across the valley south-eastward, and from there the gales have been blowing, on their way from France, a multitude of wild currents, blanketings, buffets, surges, withdrawings, impulses, every one different in voice, but all strangely subdued to a controlling fury.

And behind the wind comes the rattle of the rain on window and roof. What a tattoo it makes, like rice at a wedding as the anxious pair drive off. During the day, I have been stopped from work by this incessant summons at the pane. Getting up from the desk, I have wandered to the glass, and through its streaming greenness, as though under the sea, I have peered out at the valley, where the great boulders of leaden cloud are tumbling along, while beneath them the rain is sweeping like a cold comet's tail, spreading out, unravelling, drifting and spinning over the woods and fields. Down in the bottom I can see, in the orchard behind the farmhouse, a gleam of steel. It is the rising river, widening out, spreading beneath the apple trees and reflecting one after one until a second topsy-turvy orchard stands reflected there. The farmhouse, too, is threatened, and the master and his men are out banking up the stream to prevent the flood sweeping across the vegetable garden and over the ground floor of the old house. The pigs have been moved, and are now half-way up the hill, wired round in a narrow sleeve of the cherry orchard. Within a few hours they have nosed up the turf, looking for truffles, and a plough might have been at work there. What will be the effect on the fruit? Some say that such cultivation spoils the crop, and tends to make wood.

Down comes the rain again, even as I contemplate it. I cannot stay indoors, uncomfortable as it may be to venture out into a world blown horizontal, with trees stretching westward, rooks tossing and *skwarking* in the direction pointed out by those distracted limbs. Birds, beasts, bushes, all lean away from the wind, and appear to be urging the clouds on in their mad race, bent double with the excitement of the contest. Rain blackens my mackintosh instantly as I leave the house, and the door slams after me. I gasp, and the tang of steely water touches my tongue. Ah, it is elemental, pristine! It comes from another planet, surely, and is unknown by the

dust, the turmoil, the sedentary ways of earth and its inhabitants!

This fanciful mood is short-lived, for thought is snatched
out of my consciousness by a great, cold hand of sky. Up go
the skirts of my coat, and my beret is whipped from my head.
I dash after it, clamp it on again, to feel the wet trickle inside
and down my temples. It is futile to wear spectacles, so I take
them off, with some difficulty, for now my hands are wet and
numb. I must be content to go myopically along, groping at
the storm. But I can see enough to make out the vast shapes
of the storm, the perpetual storm that is now fourteen days in
the air, and still making speed, turning old earth over and
over, tearing out its winter garments, drenching it and
darkening it with rain, rivers of rain flowing down in skeins
across which a gleam of half light sometimes falls, with a
sullen flash of mercury or tarnished silver.

The gullies are full, and their voices open and loud. I have
just seen a water-rat far from any pond or river. He has
ventured up the hill, following against the temporary falls,
tempted perhaps by the warmth and odours from the com-
post heaps at the bottom of my ground. They are steaming in
the rain, and seem to be the only warmth for miles around.
No, I am wrong, there is a great stack of loose stuff—a
miracle that it has not blown away—left after recent threshing. There too the steam is rising, and wisps of that fragrant
vapour, together with heavier clutches of the straw itself, are
snatched up by the wind, turned with a derisive mischief,
and flung across the field to be caught in the thorny hedges,
where the straw at least hangs and shudders, while the vapour
disappears, too frail to exist in such violent circumstances.

Is something dire, eventful about to happen? The wind
grows more savage, coming down with sledge-hammer blows
that almost crush the bare trees into the ground, then following this with slant punches that lift the flattened vegetation
again and batter it in mid-air. I cannot disentangle the

J

sounds now. That onslaught might be thunder; or it might be the impact of the wind on solid objects, such as barns, slopes of the arable land, massive old oaks. Nothing seems to be static. I expect to see a tree dancing across the hill top, or an over-glutted pond rise up like a cape and burst its strings and flurry above the fields. Only, on reflection (and everything has a reflection) I know that while the wind is at this prank, uprooting and flinging broadcast every terrestrial solid, the rain is pinning it down again with arrows of water, soaking, weighting, anchoring the universe until earth and sky, human moods and personalities, past and present and future, all double their density.

I am breathless, battling against this hilarity of the heavens. I laugh, too, I see the cosmic joke. I know what it means. I see it bringing new life to the thirsty world, prodding the clods to work, bursting the seeds and tubers. 'Begin again,' it shrieks. 'This is the coming of spring. It is the sun's adventure which we herald! To work, to work in the rain!' And I turn, duck my head, and run before it, knowing that I too must obey.

IT IS USELESS to determine to carry on in my habitual, daily way, for the smell of drying hops is once again filling the countryside, and drifting in through my open windows. How much it recalls; all the autumns of my life, and particularly those two at the beginning of the last World War, 1939 and 1940, with the stark anxieties of the one, and the grim realities of the other. Through those days of magnified experience the scene here in Kent, so near the front of the battle, was saturated with this perfume of the hop, and the irony of it was almost too much to bear. It is the very breath of peace; fragrant, with a slightly sharp, metallic hint, as a rose might smell if nature had compromised and modelled its petals in gold-leaf. Or maybe the apples of Hesperides smelled so, with an other-worldly quality.

I cannot attempt to define it. There it is, a pervasive atmosphere, accompanied by the droning music of the air rushing through the draught vents of the oast-houses which I can see dotted about the landscape, their cowls adding a Slavonic touch to the scene. Night and day that drone is maintained, rising (as so many of the minor sounds of nature and humanity) gradually above the more urgent and the louder assaults upon the ear. It has become the very voice of September, more so even than that where 'in a drooping choir the small gnats mourn'. In the evenings, when the hundreds of camp fires lighted by the hop-pickers who come in their thousands from the cities and the gypsy quarters, are twinkling like sulky stars about the hill sides, and the cries of children and the barking of dogs are lifted on snatches of song, still that perfume and that droning of the oasts dominate over everything else, just as the past can often hang above the present, to darken it while enriching it.

This year the festival, the rites of autumn, is doubly picturesque because every day has been deep and timeless with sunshine, part of the amazing summer of blazing light. Here, even in my English garden in a northern latitude, I am still picking Turkey figs half as big as my fist, and biting into their luscious flesh to find it warm. Grapes too are ripening on the walls of the house, both white and black. This will be a year remembered by gardeners—and poets.

That is why the hop-gardens of Kent are so colourful too. The long aisles between the strings, sharp-pointed gothic arches of vine-shaped green, topped with the paler green of the fruits, are now full of traffic, all the odds and ends of humanity, in their odds and ends of clothing, who flock here for the picking. Old and young they are at it, bending over the bins of honey-coloured sacking, stripping the fruits from the bines, singing and chattering as they work. Along the lanes beside the gardens, usually so silent, there stand the fish-and-chip vans, the ice-cream carts, the mobile snack-bars, run by the *spivs* who loiter about the lanes, smart alecs in pointed shoes, flash suits, chokers, and harsh voices. The conflict of colours is garish, but it is opulent too, fitting symbol of the Dionysiac associations of this festival of the hop-bine.

I had to explore more closely today. I could not merely glance at it from my work-room window. So I left the urgent matters, and in a mood of half-delicious guiltiness, I walked down the hill to the farm, where the nearest cluster of oasts is now at work. Everybody there is flustered. The farmhouse is surrounded by a crowd of women and children, for there is always something wrong, or something wanted, by these townsfolk out of their true setting. The farmer's wife has put up a sort of counter outside her scullery window, and from there she ministers to the suppliants, often aided by the district nurse; for there are children with pains and damaged limbs, old folk in trouble of one kind or another, insurance card problems which the good wife refers to the 'bookers', the temporary clerks sitting in the huts in the yard, or walking about in the gardens, noting down the amount of picking done by each individual, and scoring the tally against the wages due at the end of the day. Mongrels fight the farm dogs; poached rabbits are furtively secreted into bags or capacious pockets; arguments are quelled in good nature; for good nature is the final mood after all the disputes, grievances, accidents and traffickings.

The drone of the fire draughts is now a roar. These oasts have recently been modernized. The old fireplaces, that used to burn anthracite coal openly, with pans of sulphur smouldering beside the coals, are now replaced by huge oil jets, like gigantic blowlamps, that project a blue flame into a large enclosure of bricks, whence it is spread and its heat cast upward to the drying floor some twenty feet above. That floor is now a sacred area, carefully shut off, and to be seen only through a small glass window in the door to the upper part of the kiln. On the floor of open laths is first spread a horse-hair matting. On this lies another of goat hair, and the second mat carries the hops, about five hundredweight at each drying. The process lasts for nine hours, and then the goat-hair mat is dragged out to the barn floor, and the hops shaken out. When cool, they are swept to the press with large, dustpan-shaped frames, and the press fills them into the 'pockets', packing them so tight that the filled pocket, five feet high and weighing a hundredweight and a half, is as tight as a drum. The pockets are stencilled with the farmer's name, the date, the rotation number, and the white horse of Kent (a symbol over a thousand years old).

This year a new device has been tried out with great success. It is an electrical instrument for testing the degree of dryness of the hops in the pockets. This is an important matter, for it determines the price and the readiness of the market. The farmer winds a handle on a small box containing a dynamo. From this a lead goes to two long, sharp prongs, which are thrust deep into a hop pocket, top, middle and bottom. The amount of moisture is shown on a dial, whose figures register the resistance to the small electric current created by the turning of the dynamo. This is another of the innovations of science which are breaking down so many of the age-old customs and rituals of the countryside. But I notice that there is no sentimental regret among the younger men. On the contrary, they welcome the modern touch, believing that it gives a kudos to their labour on the soil, bringing it into line with industrial work where mechanization is all. Mechanization on the land is what they want; for who that is young does not desire to be in the fashion?

IT IS IMPOSSIBLE to sit within doors this week, for all the country world is out in the harvest fields, offering up its unconscious thanksgiving, with pitchfork and rake, guttural cries to horse and tractor, shouts of laughter and mischief. It is a holy sight, and no sane person could hold aloof from it. I look out of my high window, to watch the loading of the waggons. There are four of them in the oatfield, where for the past two weeks of harsh sunshine the stooks have been drying, row upon row, opulent and spilling over. I must go down, but first, let me take a general cast of the scene, to print upon my inward eye, a wealth against the coming winter (though I suspect that the joys of winter will oust it!).

I see young Don, the eight-year-old son of our cook, struggling with a sheaf which he has dragged out from a stook and is now hauling towards the nearest waggon. I can hear his broad accent as he plays the man, and I know that when I walk through the gate of the field, two lucid grey eyes will stare with surprise at my entrance, then break into laughter that will crumple the whole of that small, mahogany face into creases, making it a mask of centenarian wisdom. He is one of those people in whom extremes meet; eight years and eighty. I never can decide which of the two figures suits him and his odd little ways.

There are several other youngsters, amongst them two girls, one in a ragged pink frock, the other smart in a blue linen overall. But the smartness is ameliorated by a filthy handkerchief tied round a knee. All of them are crazy with excitement. They dart about like terriers, shouting and screaming, while the horses flick ears at them, wondering what all the commotion may mean, and hoping that it will have some effect upon the plague of flies.

The men of the farm work on oblivious of all this. Indeed, they are almost as hilarious. Here is no grudging labour, about which we hear so much in a too-political world. These fellows are absorbed in the day's work. It seems to be no longer work in the trade union sense, with employer and employed. The farmer and his two sons are here also, with no mark to distinguish them from their men. All are at it, heaving, bending, tossing. The movement is ancient. It is part of a ritual that began when neolithic man first turned from hunting to the scratching of the soil, and the settlement in one place. The way that pitchfork is held and flourished must be several thousand years old. It comes from Chaldea, the small holding just outside the gates of the Garden of Eden, established when the Curse was first pronounced; the curse that is proving to be our salvation, as we expiate its cause.

But I am wandering into the past, and today everything is in the present; all summer in a day, and all the wealth of the earth, and the granary of mankind, here in the toss of a few forks, and piling up into a golden house on the waggons. Now one of them is fully loaded, and the tandem of horses is given the signal. Heave, heave again, and with a clotty jolt the great galleon moves. It seems to stop again, but that is only the inertia of the load, which swings back, then forward, as the waggon beneath it creeps along the stubble. The carter cracks his whip, and shouts some unintelligible syllables. Then he stops to light his pipe, and moves after his charge, which is steadily, maternally floating, like a woman heavy with child, along under the hedgerow, passing perilously near the row of gigantic oaks, but just missing their boughs. The shadows rush over the load, flecks of sun sprinkle it with further gold; gold upon gold, wealth amassing wealth. How it swings, dips, hesitates, dips, and swings again. Is it part of another Spanish Armada, coming up from Peru, the land of the Incas, loaded with ingots? It looks that way, moving over

the bare field, now an ocean of wide space, but with undula-
tion enough to keep this full-breasted creature somewhat
over-conscious of its dignity as it floats so proudly down to the
lower gate and the lane.

Now I have joined the children. 'Hallo, Betty!' I
exclaim, to the girl in the blue overall and with the bandaged
leg. 'Hurt your knee?' She looks puzzled by my question.
Then light breaks over her face. 'Naw!' she cries. 'I dawn't
want ter lose me 'andkerchief while I'm 'arvestin'!'

Don meanwhile has dragged a sheaf across my shoes, too
intent to notice my arrival, until he bangs into my legs. This
is a matter for the utmost abandonment to mirth. It is the
spark to the powder barrel. All the children explode, dancing
around me, then rolling on the stubble, helpless and blinded.
I stand like a rock, a monument of solemnity. 'Ou!' shouts
one of the sons of the farmer, thinking I am embarrassed, and
mistaking the part I am playing in the game of harvest-
home; 'Oi! get out there, less muckin' about!' And he lunges
forward, seizes the shrieking blue-linen, and hoists her up on
the back of the front horse of the second waggon. The great
shire-mare does not even look round. A flicker goes over her
roan skin. That is all. The child is perched up there like a
little Hindoo on the head of an elephant. She gasps for
breath, shivers, then decides she likes it, and elects to stay
there.

I pick up Don, my eight-year-old friend made up by sun
and laughter to carry the wrinkles of eighty, hand him to one
of the men on the load, and in a second he is high above the
top of the hedges, sitting there and bouncing in the spring of
the gold. A bronze-tinted dust rises round him, which the
afternoon sunlight catches and turns to fire. There he
smoulders, and a butterfly joins him, flicking round his head.
'See that butterfly, Don?' I cry, with my head thrown back
as I stare up at the pyre of light with the infant throned in the
middle of it. ' 'Taint a butterfly; it's a moth,' he retorts,

snatching a handful of corn stalks and throwing it down at me. This brings the wrath of the loader down upon him. 'Oi! Doan't muck that pilin' about or I'll chuck ye down!' A horrifying threat, which the boy takes for what it is worth.

Now this waggon too begins to move, and my heart is in my mouth as I watch the child on top of the load swinging about like a stone in a catapult. But he is safe enough, for the man behind him has put a hand on his shoulder, and thus the grouping is completed. The statuary moves off, part of the carnival of the year, the girl on the horse, the man and boy on the monolith of gold. The sun is behind them, going down too, and the great heat of the day is falling. Down to the gate we all follow, and half the harvest will then be in, with tomorrow also a day.

ONE OF THE greater pleasures of passing into the autumn of life comes from our increasing ability to make comparisons. Our reference library of memories is so much larger. The fact that we have to carry this library with us night and day, wherever we may be, makes no doubt for a certain slowing down of the pace of our lives; but we are none the worse for that.

> 'Grow old along with me;
> The best is yet to be,'

said Robert Browning, through the mouth of Rabbi Ben Ezra, and he was likely to know, for had he not lived life to the full, with love, fame and genius deployed with an almost extravagant gesture during his years of youth and maturity?

I have been consoling myself with thoughts of this kind for the past two months, since returning from a holiday in Italy, which included a first visit to Venice. While I was there I found myself crushed to earth under the burden of such rich experiences. I might have been a gothic invader, intruding into the great Roman Empire spear in hand, with clotted hair and the savage gods of Valhalla seething in my brain. I found myself a barbarian, gazing at the superb past, yes, and at the present too, as I drifted about the alleys and canals of the immortal City of the Sea. For the genius of Rome has never died. It works today, as it worked through the Middle Ages and the Renaissance, providing a sort of ground base of design for all the arts, the politics, the dogmas and handicrafts, which through the succeeding centuries have been weaving the fabric of this almost fabulous entity, this Idea, this civilization, which we call *Italy*.

Small wonder that all people, of all nations and times, who are moved by an ideal of something to be made that shall be beautiful and *right,* crave to visit that land as pilgrims. I recall the description written by Goethe in his autobiography, *Dichtung und Warheit* (Poetry and Truth), where as a young man on the threshold of fame and maturity, he crossed the Alps, and looking south across the Plain of Lombardy, realized that he was faced with the promised land whose peoples and works had fed his studious days since infancy. 'In such moments,' said Goethe, 'it seems to me as if a man has no power to make a decision in himself, but is rather governed and determined by earlier impressions.'

That is precisely what I felt throughout my first stay in northern Italy. I saw what I saw, not with the naked eye, but through the diminishing glass, as though I were looking through the wrong end of the telescope of my own past intellectual and aesthetic experiences. Thus it was that I found Venice somewhat smaller than I had anticipated. At least, it was so at first. I stood, during half an hour on that first evening, on the Ponte dell'Accademia, staring up and down the Grand Canal, and finding myself faintly dismayed by the sense of *homeliness* of the scene. The palaces were lower, the Canal narrower, than those which had inhabited my imagination throughout my life, reflected from the pages of the poets and the canvases of the painters. Was *this* the reality which had fed the eyes of Canaletto and Turner? The question came with a cold breath of disillusion, and I felt an appalling sense of loneliness seize me, as though I had been cheated.

I was to learn within a day or two, that this sense of cheat was only the loss of that cloistral self-concern which hangs like a dark curtain before all our pre-conceptions, to dim the full light of experience. Next morning I woke early, and saw a sun shaft reflected from the canal below my bedroom window. It fluttered about the painted ceiling of the room like a transparent butterfly; and as though keeping time with it I heard the *nudge-nudge* of a gondola, as it nosed against the steps of the water-gate of the house, to which it was moored. A canary in a window of the palazzo, a few yards across the canal, was shouting its golden song. Swifts skated up and down between the buildings, tweeting as they went, shrill and wildly excited. The maid knocked at the door, entered with morning tea, and set it down with a gesture and a greeting like a passage from an opera of Mozart, every syllable, every movement graceful and implicit with courtesy. I was in another world. It was the world in which I had thought I had been during so many years of illusion. This was the reality, and it was better than my error. And the reason why it was better was because it was human, natural, unpretentious.

I believe that I could never cease to contemplate and to write about this quality of naturalness in the Italians and their way of life, that ancient way which has been handed down intact for two thousand years. It is the ground-base of everything they do, and everything they have done, from the building of the Palace of the Doges (surely one of the wonders of the world), to the mending of a pair of shoes or the handing of a cup of coffee. The act, no matter how magnificent (as when Tintoretto painted his colossal pictures), no matter how small (as when the maid brought the morning tea), is always an act of courtesy. How acceptable that is. How fully it explains why mankind comes and returns again and again to Italy for refreshment of body, mind and soul. So it was with me. I felt the stain of war years bleaching out of my mind. I looked next morning at the Grand Canal again, with its lining of Renaissance palaces, its gondolas floating like slices of black melon; and the Canal was wider, the palaces more ducal.

That was the beginning of my change of heart. I still had not begun to explore. I still had no inkling of the vast riches that lay ahead, not only in the museums and galleries, but in the odd corners of alley and water-way. It was the latter that first compelled me, stamping the authority of Venice upon my spirit. A mooring post, a boss over a doorway, a shop sign. These were the signature of an ancient civilization, for my first study.

HAVING BEEN TO Venice; having at last seen that fabulous city and imposed reality upon the fable, I am now making my way back there in recollection. It is an intermittent occupation, indulged in willy-nilly by sheer magnetic attraction, during working days and wakeful nights. Much of it is confusion, the confusion of riches that poured in upon my imagination and senses during my short stay there. The motions of my mind are like those of a medieval miser gloating over his ducats, running them through his fingers in and out of the coffer, too dazed with a hungry satiety to be able to count them one by one.

That is why I cannot, at this stage, get back to Venice itself. I am still at the approaches, the distant approaches too. There I must remain for awhile, waiting, as it were, for the mental traffic block to sort itself out. Meanwhile, I think of a day by the Lake of Como.

Picture any warm April day in north Europe, when 'half the world a bridegroom is, and half the world a bride'. And pile upon that ravishment the scene in the foothills of the Italian Alps, where those superb rocks, still scarfed with snow here and there round their stony summits, come down fold upon fold to the lakeside. And on every other hill a campanile in the Byzantine manner, with a chapel beside it like a camel tied to a post. The buildings are ancient enough. Some of them date from within the first millenium of the Christian faith, and they stand there weathered to the colour of a child's flesh, or the petal of a hedge rose; enduring a reversal of the processes of time, growing younger and fresher as the centuries pass. Do they not thus symbolize more truly the religion which they celebrate?

151

Half-way up the right-hand shore of the lake, where the two legs meet, stands or rather perches a small village called Varenna. The hills almost push it into the water, and its streets and steps (for most of its traffic is done on cobbled slopes with hundreds of steps of differing height and depth; a martyrdom to the muscles of the calves, and to the soles of the feet), cling to the rockside, the squat-roofed houses stuck there like swallows' nests, or rather (because of their tints) like Joseph's coat of many colours draped beside the well while the brothers dispute.

One day we took the weekly motor-bus which goes up from this village to another four thousand feet up. The progress was in low gear all the way, and we stopped from time to time to negotiate hair-pin bends, or to await a passenger who would come along in a leisurely mood, carrying a crate of hens, or some more unlikely burden. One elderly peasant, wrinkled and burned by the years as much as by the weather, wearing a black hat and suit with a slight patina of dust over them, carried a Woolworthian suit-case of cardboard. With this on his knees, he passed the time by opening it and reading the labels of the gramophone records with which it was filled. This pleasant incongruity almost withdrew my attention from the passing, or dropping scene. For we climbed and climbed, while a column of steam rose from the radiator. First one side, then the other side faced the lake, which was withdrawing itself so that its surface became a crinkled sheet of linen, with a fly crawling on it and leaving a trail of arrow-shaped light. That was the *vaporetto,* the steamboat which knitted its way across the lake from morning to night, as though trying to darn it together. Truly, from this height, the waters looked like a hole, through which we could see the sky.

Then at last we reached the mountain village, which like all mountain villages was deluged in silence, a pall of silence that came down like an invisible hand and muffled it. We spoke to a workman who was cementing a flat patch in a garden. He told us he was making a dance floor! And we heard all about his war years as a prisoner of the Germans. He crossed his wrists, to indicate servitude. Like all the waiters in France, so most of the Italians to whom I spoke, had been resistance men, and martyrs for their country. That only endeared them the more to me, because it showed an aspiration after heroism, a salutary thing in this materialistic world.

After some refreshment, to recover from the vertigo of the bus journey, we began to climb over the remaining height, round a spur that should lead us to the head of the next valley, down which we could descend to the next village along the lake side. That would be a day's walking.

How much more it was. A day's walking, certainly, as our poor limbs reminded us from time to time; but an eternity in experience of beauty, mystery, awe. There is something about heights which alone is a stimulation to the spirit. There comes over one a sense of earliness, of being in the very morning of time and the youth of the world, with humanity just beginning its career, suckled on innocence and rapture, and lifting up its head among the frosty stars and laughing in the light. Granted all that; granted the recognition of escape from routine, and crowds, and politics; then add the rest. But how to describe, even to enumerate that rest? I cannot do it, any more than I can begin to approach Venice, which is my ultimate destination, essay by essay, for perhaps the next few decades of literary activity.

I can only hint by symbols. I recall the first stage of the climb, after leaving the cobbled paths of the village, with the dogs and hens, and two infants with flaxen hair, blue eyes, and coal-black feet. The mountain rose above us, a steady sweep of scrubland with patches of birch and pine, dry-walls and here and there the channels of rivulets now stony trucks, because of the drought and the snowless winter. But what

K

else? A paradise garden of flowers. With even my small knowledge, I could count a few of their kinds; first, the general carpet of white crocuses, broken with flesh-coloured cyclamen, and starred with gentians and anemones of a vivid, metallic blue with white centres. And here and there the carpet was chequered by a patch of hellebore, or Christmas rose, its huge and elaborate leaves hung with the sulky blossoms of silken velvet, with their bilious tints. An impressive sight; so impressive that we almost ignored the myriad other and more familiar flowers, the commoners of a Wordsworthian humility, the campanula, columbine, the worts and the daisied stars, the orchises and the ivies. And there, performing a wild ballet over this carpet, touching it with kisses yet not touching it, hovered a company of swallow-tail butterflies; and the rarer variety too, as their stripes indicated. We took off our hats, and our sunglasses, and gazed, and gazed. 'And still the wonder grew.'

The lake below us, a waft of unreality like blue smoke; two peasant women stumping down the slope, each beneath a load of hay which she carried in a cornucopia-shaped basket on her back, with the point in her waist, and the contents towering above her head: a man cutting the emerald grasses with a scythe: these must suffice as an indication of the time and the place. And I would add an eagle, hovering and gliding over the mountain top; nothing to do with us, nothing to do with earth at all. And finally, the songs rising from the ravine, where the trees closed together, and the green deepened; the songs of the nightingales, raving at midday.

IF THE CAP FITS

An old friend, a historical dramatist, recently died and left me his books, manuscripts, and a curious old cap with a peak that went all round it. This cap was the colour of dust. 'If it fits,' he said in his will, 'you will find it of uncommon value.'

The day after receiving that inheritance I went for a walk by the Medway. Standing by the bridge in Maidstone I felt a cold wind coming up the river. It sighed round me and dimmed the spring sunshine. I saw a distant group of daffodils beyond the Palace Gardens tremble and shake their bells in a shivering fit that communicated itself to me also. I put my hand in my overcoat pocket and found the old historian's cap which I put on my cold head. It fitted.

That was much warmer. I looked along the river again, wondering if the daffodils were still shivering. They had vanished. And many other things had vanished. The Market Place on the bank opposite the palace had disappeared completely with all its clobber of sheds, railings and cinder-tracks. I saw there only a stretch of water spread from the flooded stream which was tumbling past me and carrying down a dozen royal swans at a vigorous pace past the palace.

I had no time to wonder about this transformation, because it was followed by others. I was no longer standing on the bridge. Under my feet was a broken esplanade still muddied with the traffic of craftsmen and waggons. And the mud was greyish, streaked with iron, out of which protruded odd pieces of shaped or broken stone. The sun was still shining, however, and the chilly wind which had persuaded me to put on the historian's cap had subsided. Sticking out of the flood water was a gorse bush marking the hedge on the riverside path on the opposite bank. It made a little cushion of gold reflected in the flood in which it stood, and the sun smote it and burnished it so that it blazed.

Then I turned round and in that instant realized that something superhuman had taken place. Before me I saw Maidstone Parish Church of All Saints, but it shone like ivory, and beyond it shone another group of superb masonry with an embattled gateway tower, a river tower, a great house with yet another tower and, over this last, a large ecclesiastical flag drooping from a mast. And as I looked the wind rose again and out flew the flag, white and gold, with a figure of blue in it, the river ripples glittered, and the gorse bush blazed and the kingly swans sailed on like white galleons down the stream.

I stared and stared again, all my sense quickened. I could smell the incense of fruit-wood fires, and I could hear a music of plain-song sung by a choir in the church. It came with a sudden swell as someone opened a side door, and then it receded again as the door closed. A man approached me from the church, stopping once or twice to contemplate and to stroke various massive slabs of masonry still in process of being shaped and carved. His feet crunched on the chips every time he moved nearer to me. I could see beyond him a little group of men in unfamiliar clothes. They were working beneath some scaffolding that still surrounded the north transept.

He looked at me curiously as he came abreast, and stopped. I could see his eyes scrutinizing my clothes as mine were scrutinizing his. We were both puzzled but were too polite to comment.

By now I had seen enough to realize that my old historian's cap had begun to play tricks with time. I suspected that it had carried me out from the twentieth century. There in front of me was evidence enough; a glory of stonework with a shining roof and the Archbishop's Palace in all its splendour with the episcopal flag flying in the breeze of another age. The stranger's first word confirmed my suspicion.

'God be with you, sir,' he said, with an accent that made me think immediately of the rich human poetry of Geoffrey Chaucer. The greeting was quite simple and unselfconscious, and I returned it in the same spirit. He smiled at me and a little crease of marble dust on his cheek slid over the skin like a glove over a hand.

'You come to Maidstone on a happy day, sir,' he said.

'What day is this, Master Mason?' I inquired. Then, encouraged by his friendliness, I decided to complete my question. 'And what *year* is this?'

This addition to my question caused his eyes to grow sharp. Obviously he was puzzled, but an instant later I could see that he took my request as a formality intended to conjure up in words the whole ceremonial of the occasion. He replied with a rhetorical relish, and thus betrayed a mood and social attitude obviously not belonging to the twentieth century.

'Stranger,' he said in tones like a flourish of trumpets, 'today is a proud one for the great Archbishop and for all our guildsmen who have worked for him in the building of this church and palace. This year of our Lord 1397 will be remembered through the ages by all the folk of Kent and all strangers who come to our royal county because of the work completed here today. This church and palace, this college of learning, are a noble foundation in perpetual stone, a monument of craftsmen and all that is beautiful in our human family, all that is made by brain and hands, master and man, in this English society to which we all are subject under God and King.'

He held out his hand to take mine, and I advanced a pace, taking off my cap as I did so, for he had doffed his. Instantly the scene changed. The stonemason had vanished, and the fourteenth century with him. I saw the squalid Market Place across the oil-fouled river. The stench of petrol fumes blew down from the bridge above me. I was back in the twentieth century, with the historian's cap in my hand.

I SUPPOSE THAT a passion for walking in woods is universal. Primitive man began his life beneath, and perhaps in the branches of trees, if we are to believe some of the theories of science. Whatever we believe, however, we have this instinct in our hearts, that to plunge into a wood is to enter once again the world of magic into which we are born and in which we spend our childhood and youth. In those early years we carry with us from we know not where, primordial urges and intuitions which make us respond instantly to the mysterious twilights, the gleams and shadows, that lurk for ever in the thickets wherever a dozen or more trees are gathered together.

Once submerged beneath those shades, we are spellbound. Our personal concerns, the frets and fevers of the world, the sophistications and veneers which our social contacts put upon us, all these are blotted out, and we tread with the stealth and anxious rapture of wild creatures; simple, intent, watchful. This attitude, and this relationship between mankind and the forests of the earth, have inevitably led to a mythology and a symbolism in which are lodged as many of our arboreal experiences as are capable of being captured in the imagery of words, and thus made static and memorable. The myth, for example, of the Forest of Broceliande has about it a universality which must appeal to child and adult alike, with its delicious terrors, instantly recognizable and to be savoured on the imagination as things fabulous, but perennially familiar in those estates of the mind, where so much of both our waking and sleeping lives is spent. What thrills creep upon our skin whenever we read the snatch of poetry in which the chief figurement is an image of the woods!

Think of the wonderful opening of George Meredith's poem
The Woods of Westermain:

> 'These are the woods of Westermain;
> Enter ye who dare!'

and of the wizardry that follows, spellbinding, comparable to
that practised by Merlin in the oak forests of ancient Britain,
when the rites of the trees played an important part in the
making and breaking of kingships. Indeed, the influence of
the trees, and their human guardians, was one of the leading
forces in the articulation of early human society. Sir James
Frazer, in *The Golden Bough*, opens the book with a chapter
called 'The King of the Wood', in which he recalls Turner's
picture of the little woodland lake of Nemi in the Alban hills
below Rome: wooded heights, whose trees were infested with
that elfin parasite, the mistletoe (the golden bough itself).
Those opening pages by Frazer are the nearest approach in
words that I can recall to a picture by Claude, a painter who
had the genius of woods in his blood; deep, slumbering wells
of verdure within whose magnificent umbrage the eternal
adventure of beauty lay in wait.

But whoever was a freeman of this particular realm of
inspiration, painter, poet or musician, he had within the
scope of his consciousness an enlargement of self that made
him freeman of the most majestic and at the same time the
most tender and intimate of all the vast personality of our
mother earth. Innumerable lists could be made of the masters
in all the arts for whom contact with the trees was an ever-
urgent necessity. That tormented spirit Beethoven found his
principal solace in walking about in the woods outside
Vienna, muttering to himself, stopping to make entries in his
immortal notebooks, or in his more peaceful moments reading in that favourite book of his, called *Sturm's Reflections*.
No doubt his tumultuous genius was soothed by the quaint

moralizings of the old German Pastor, whose reflections were once so much sought after. It is almost amusing to read such a passage as the following, to picture Beethoven reflecting upon it, as he trod up and down to the swishing sound of fallen beech leaves and the crisper crunching of the dried mast, and from that reflection to translate the humble words into a movement of the Pastoral Symphony.

'Thus has the all-wise Creator formed an admirable system of solid and fluid matter in order to give life and growth to those trees which adorn our plains, which lend their friendly shade to our flocks, to our shepherds and to our cottages and which afterwards serve so many purposes useful to man. Here we discover a wisdom which never fails, whilst it prescribes to nature laws in certain prospects, immutable, which act without interruption under the eye of Providence.'

What is perhaps most charming is the contrast between the close piety of the literary phrase which Beethoven fed upon, and the enormous gesture, like a brush stroke by Michael Angelo, of the musical phrase of the composer. But that contrast is reconciled, resolved within the notation of the woodlands. Such are their magic and their discipline. At least in our temperate zones, the forests have this authority, by which they bring all that enter their cloisters into a mood of reconciliation. I would coin a word for it, and call it 'sylvanity', a word intended to convey the all-embracing green-ness into which we enter at the threshold of even the smallest coppice, to partake there of this potion, chlorophyllic in effect. It is more than the essence of a colour, for it has the power not only to refresh eyes made gritty by the dust of daily life, but to percolate through the inmost reaches of our personality with its gentle lippings of leaf tone, the very music of light and shade and the immortal dyes of earth itself.

I read recently a book called *The Triumph of the Tree,* by John Stewart Collis, in which the author set out to write a history of the whole of this relationship between man and the tree. He considers the mythology of trees, he pictures the primordial world during the genesis of the coal beds, he shows the emergence of mankind, a timid experiment with a curiously unprotected biped cradled in the forests which at that stage of earth's story stretched like a hirsute pelt through all the lowlands of the dry land to threaten even ocean itself. 'We began amongst trees,' says Mr Collis, 'can we imagine now what it was like living in the days of that beginning? We can have some idea; for though the corrosions of Time do carve incredible changes on the creatures and the landscapes of the earth, there are some things which repeat themselves so closely as seeming to ignore the passage of centuries.'

That repetition is for ever taking place in our hearts and minds whenever we walk in woods, to partake of their divine refreshment through our five senses, and that sixth sense which is greatest of all, that sense which recognizes the eternal Substance which is the living God whose sculpturing Hand never ceases from shaping anew these green cathedrals with their massive pillars and their microscopic ornamentation of bud, and tumbled husk to serve as a carpet of quietness and sanctity.

SHADOWS IN THE HAMLET

THE TROUBLE WITH the townsman who goes to live in the country is that he tends to wander about with his head in the air, sniffing the four seasons with an ecstatic nose, and neglecting the more basic elements of which nature, and human nature, are composed. I find myself continually at fault in that way, and just lately I have had a timely rap to remind me that the serpent who played so important a part in the history of the family of Man, entered that history by way of the garden, and set about his machinations with a tree in the foreground.

No, the countryside is not always innocent and serene, and at the moment I am somewhat anxiously conscious of this because of events taking place, or said to be taking place, in our hamlet.

Two of our oldest inhabitants, deep-rooted natives, are brothers who live together in a disused beerhouse. It is a picturesque building, of wood and Kentish red tiles. To judge from its proportions (and that is about all there is left of it) it was put up in the latter end of the eighteenth century, for the angles are elegant, though the fabric is slattern. Weatherboards are missing here and there, the gaps being stuffed with

163

sacking mucked with an application of tar, or boarded over with lids of cube sugar boxes. One end of the crusted old roof is in a shameful state, and three sheets of tattered corrugated iron cover the otherwise naked rafters. The front door is nailed up and a string of scarlet runners grows across it in summer. Its winter adornment is the dry and rattling pods and stems of last year's beans. On one panel of the door is a tin-plate advertisement for Mazawattee Tea. It must have been nailed up there in 1880, to judge from the typography. The windows are wall-eyed with dirt, those that still have glass in them. The rest are merely sockets, filled with bits of odd wood and sacking. In one of them the sacking is augmented with a bird's nest, to add to the blindness. The front garden is a mass of old box bushes overgrowing what was once a path, where brambles and nettles contend, only too successfully, with a few attenuated cabbage stalks. The fence on to the lane is mostly down, a fragment of it still leaning outward. This too would have fallen had not there been a tree to support it. The tree, too, is probably glad of the prop, for it is very old, very moss-sodden, furrowed with grey ribs along every bough. But each year in May it puts out a few soft blossoms, and each autumn still fewer sour damsons.

The general effect is perhaps ornamental, but wholly sordid. The hamlet is not proud of this small holding; but nothing can be done about it while the brothers, the two freeholders, survive along with their damson tree. They, however, put out no white blossoms in the spring. They keep a perpetual autumn, and their fruit is everlastingly sour. One of them, the elder, is said to be—*you know what!* That is the phrase. He looks it. He is always muffled up in a sort of reefer jacket, with an old cap on his head. Cap and head are so much of a piece, that it is impossible to differentiate one from the other. They are of the same colour, a smokey greyish-brown, half shiny with the natural greases that accumulate wherever animal life continues for long in one place. He is blind in one eye, and the ear on that side is stuffed with a wad of what was once cotton-wool. He wears a scarf, perhaps because of this affliction, and thus his head is only half apparent, like an egg in a cup. But an egg in its cup, so smooth, so neat and dapper, is an incongruous simile for this old man, because he is an object that one associates with fogs, mosses, composts of all sorts.

His younger brother is the bread-winner, and is more recognizable as a member of society. He has two eyes, and obviously shaves from time to time. His clothes have the appearance of being removable. And he makes contact with his neighbours, doing odd jobs such as hacking down brambles, tidying up bits of overgrown waste ground. But his main means of support is his licence to sell tobacco and cigarettes. And it is this that has led to the shadow over the hamlet.

I first heard of the trouble from the gamekeeper, who came to my back door with a rabbit. 'Have you 'eard about the burglary?' he asked. He is always a soft-voiced man, due perhaps to his solitary life. He seemed reluctant to use the dramatic word. It sounded more like the buzz of a passing bee, than a reference to housebreaking. I got him to repeat it; and he blushed. Then, in an embarrassed whisper, he told me that three people, two men and a woman (he emphasized, 'And a woman, mind you!') had gone round to the back of the old beerhouse (its licence long since fallen into history), forced their way through the half door, and robbed the old brother of half his store of cigarettes. The police had been informed, at the small town five miles away, and an inspector had been over on a motor-bike. But nothing more. Sympathy for the poor old chap was seasoned with indignation that *foreigners*, by that was meant squatting fruit-pickers, some of whom had remained on in the hop-picker huts after the autumn season, should be allowed to 'get away with it'.

Next day, I passed the elder brother by the pond on the green. He was standing staring into its opaque surface of weeds with his one inflamed and angry eye. I murmured some words of sympathy. The eye flashed by me like a light-house beam, and passed round again. There was no humane contact. I took it as the mariners take their warning beam, a sign of rocks ahead and a lee shore. 'Eh?' grunted the old brother; and returned to his weed gazing.

Two days later (rumour is leisurely in our hamlet), the domestic help, a comely and vigorous married woman, brought the subject afresh into the house. 'Wicked business, I call it!' she said. 'What's the police doing, I want to know? Them poor old chaps got their living to make, ain't they? To be held up with a revolver, too! Why, it ain't civilized, leastways in old England it ain't. Might be living in them foreign parts you see on the films. I don't know what we be coming to, I'm sure.' She saw red with anger, and fear. And to my surprise, I saw that it would not do for me to make my usual weekly journey to London, leaving the house solely in charge of one dear companion and the Corgi dog. I should first have to get this rumour removed, and the shadow cleared from our hamlet.

AN ENCOUNTER IN VENICE

Coming out of the Hotel Savoia Yolanda, on the Riva degli Schiavoni, I knew that something unusual was about to happen to me. It was the twelfth of December, a dark and angry day with a savage wind rushing up the Bacino di San Marco from the open sea. The clouds above it were pressing down almost to touch the water, and the water shrank from the touch. Snow was falling. Snow in Venice!

Impossible to find shelter; impossible to turn back into the half-heated hotel: for I was restless. Some strange disturbance of mind was driving me out into the mad weather, willy-nilly. I was fortunate, perhaps, in having brought my kit down from the Dolomites, though without the protection of my mountain boots I might have been forced to possess my soul in patience, remaining within the chilly lounge and gazing unadventurously out upon the snow-covered Riva and the sullen waters beyond.

I had a scarf as big as a shawl, and I tied it over my beret and tucked it in under the collar of my greatcoat. Thus

167

protected, I walked before the wind toward the Canale Grande. Before the Doge's Palace the snow piled up where the wind had gone insane. Men were clearing a way through to the Piazza, and I trod this miniature cutting in order to escape from the fury of the weather. The pigeons in the Square were not without succour, for a number of children were about, feeding them with bread and scraps from beneath their capes. The hungry and bewildered birds fought and scrambled, kicking up little flurries of snow in their fury. I walked round the Square under the Colonnade, past the Cathedral and along the top, thus escaping much of the wind and most of the snow. But venturing out again into the alleys, I was glad of the comfort of my climbing boots, for the snow lay thick, and the wind blew with even fiercer venom because of its confinement between the ancient buildings. It was as though a battle were raging between the elements of nature and the spirit of history. And for the moment, the former was likely to win.

My wits bemused by the cold and the maniacal music of the wind, I struggled on with bent head, hardly conscious of my goal. But somehow, at the back of my mind, was a purpose whose origin I could not account for. I was making for the Palazzo Rezzonico, on the left bank of the Canale, beyond the Ponte dell'Accademia. And what was my reason for this? It was connected with the day of the year. The twelfth of December. Suddenly, my wits clearing as I stood aside to let a number of muffled folk pass over one of the myriad foot-bridges, I knew what was at the back of my mind. It was the anniversary of the death of the poet Robert Browning, who came back in his old age to visit his son, who had settled here as a married man. That was in 1889, with the poet seventy-seven years of age, still eager, still planning a new home where he could produce yet more verse to add to his magnificent swan song of *Asolando*, where he maintained the old affirmations by which he had lived.

'I truly am, at last!
For a veil is rent between
Me and the truth which passed
Fitful, half-guessed, half seen,
Grasped at—not gained, held fast.'

With that vigour and resolution in him, he must have died reluctantly. The chill had taken him suddenly, and within a few days, lying fevered in that front mezzanine room in a corner of the Palazzo Rezzonico, looking down the Canale towards the Bridge, he was forced to give up the world which still held him entranced by its drama. He died young in heart; and to die young is to die unwillingly, with life a barely tasted feast.

I could see now that the emotion had been haunting me, filling my hidden self where all the sources of energy and creative effort lie. Only at this moment, as I stood pressed against the rail above some snow-filled barges, waiting for the steps to the bridge to clear, did this obsession rise to my thinking mind. I could not resist. My pilgrimage, after all, was self-commanded. Behind it was a lifetime of devotion to a man of genius; one whose birth, both in place and social station, had been identical with my own; whose gifts and interests too I understood and emulated. To have a hero in youth is to have some influence that never quite loses its magic, though as we mature and grow old, we see the feet of clay, the grossnesses, and much of the pretension. My only too sagacious contemplation of a shrunken enthusiasm served at this moment to add to my mood of piety, touching it with remorse. I saw again how lonely the central years of our lives can become, with the gods of our youth thrown down, and the deeper understanding of age not yet grown compassionate enough to erect them again, with the feet of clay exchanged for gold; the gold of our own riches won in experience.

L

A flurry of snow blew from the steps of the bridge into my face, waking me from my reverie, and showing the way clear. I walked on, still head bent, for in these alleys and up these smaller canals, the wind was striking in all directions, with steely sword thrusts that brought to my memory some long-forgotten lines from *In a Gondola*:

'What if the Three should catch at last
Thy serenader? While there's cast
Paul's cloak about my head, and fast
Gian pinions me, Himself has past
His stylet thro' my back; I reel;
And . . . is it Thou I feel?'

The ruffians were surely at me now, twitching at my garments, seeking handhold and a spot of mortal weakness where the blade could press. I shivered as I battled forward. But it was still forward, and undefeated. In a gondola, indeed! I looked down at the canal after I had crossed the Accademia and the small canal by the Casa Stephani leading out to the Canale Grande by the Traghetto, the old public ferry. I knew that house, with its little garden and hen-run between the lower hall and the water-gate where the seventeenth-century bell still hung, and the mooring-post thrust out of the water like the head of Neptune's sceptre, its gay colours draped with mosses and mildew. There was a gondola tied up now. The black cabin hood had been removed, and the vessel was completely filled with snow, so that the boat might have been a funeral barge, with a white shroud above the dead. No 'moth's kiss first' today, so many years after. The contrast of the scene, with the recalled lyric of the Venetian poem written by the ardent young poet after his first visit to Venice, was almost too much for my nerves. I was already keyed up by the fight against the storm, and the contrast of this struggle with the melancholy serenity of my deeper mood of recollection of the poet's death. I could have wept. Instead, I spoke the lines to myself as I looked down the familiar canal at the snow-filled gondola.

> 'The moth's kiss, first;
> Kiss me as if you made believe
> You were not sure, this eve,
> How my face, your flower, had pursed
> Its petals up; so, here and there
> You brush it, till I grow aware
> Who wants me, and wide open burst.'

Fire and ice; the now and the hereafter! Touched by these antinomies, I wandered on again, my heart filled with that desperation which takes us when we encounter emotions too big for our imagination to master. Thus temporarily distraught, I walked along the Calle del Traghetto, and of course came to a blind end opening on the Canale Grande. Turning back down the lane, passing again the street door of the Casa Stephani, I crossed the small square in front of the shabby old church, passed over two more canals, and at last came to the Rezzonico.

The gate was unlocked, but nobody being about, I hesitated before entering the museum. But it was foolish to wait in the cold and the snow. I stamped the snow from my boots, and went in.

Now I knew that I was not truly in command of myself, for as though being conducted by an invisible usher, I walked forward along the great tiled floors, the nails in my boots clattering and waking echoes to which there was no response. Then down to a mezzanine floor hardly above water-level, along several low corridors, I blindly followed the guide who may have been called Instinct, Monomania, Trance. I was thus led to the room where sixty years ago the old poet so reluctantly gave up the ghost; sixty years ago to the day. I am not experienced in the ways, and the laws, of that other world, that purgatory where spirits wait for their final assignment in the household of eternity. I know enough, however, not to have been surprised that on this day of anniversary, which recalled the rending and the anguish of an unwilling departure from this world of flesh and blood, I should see a stoutish figure standing at the low window in the corner of the room, resting one foot up on the panelled sill, while he examined a cigar which he was about to top with a little knife set with mother-of-pearl. His hands were podgy, and he wore a ring on each of his fourth fingers, one set with onyx, the other with a cornelian, cut for sealing.

He looked up as I entered, and I stared into a pair of dark brown eyes, somewhat hooded with age. His nose was large, with spread nostrils. The mouth was hidden behind grizzled whiskers and moustache, but I caught a flash of discoloured teeth as he smiled. His cheeks were podgy too, and gleamed rosily in the water-reflected light that moved mysteriously about the room. He seemed to know me, not only in the present, but also in my past, for he spoke at once, in tones thickened but brisk. 'Ah! I was expecting a caller. Today is important, for I have a bag to pack. But tell me first: is Dulwich where it was; the wood where Pauline walked, and I first saw Shelley plain? You learned your nature lore in that small school, as I did too. I suspect that all poets have the one instruction, various though they be. So small, yet so vast; we never learn enough, or hardly begin to learn. I have found that true, after nearly eight decades. Another Christmas is coming, and here I am again in Venice, where once. . . .' But he stopped, hesitated, and without shame or self-consciousness put his hand before his eyes, moved to tears by the recollection of what he had lost. Recovering his poise, he seemed to forget my presence, and quoted to himself some lines from his poem *Christmas Eve*, as though to argue himself back to cheerfulness and acceptance.

'Seeing death come and choose about me,
And my dearest ones depart without me.
No! love which, on earth, amid all the shows of it,
Has ever been seen the sole good of life in it,
The love, ever growing there, spite of the strife in it,
Shall rise, made perfect, from death's repose of it!'

He paused again, and incongruously went on with the preparation of his cigar, turning to look out of the window at the snow falling like a net curtain across the Canale Grande; falling and blowing out in great billowing folds that flapped against the palaces on the other side. Then he turned to me where I stood deferentially. His voice was still shaken with emotion, but a note of triumph and a certain defiance strengthened it.

'This is the thing we seek, at the end as in the beginning. It is Power; the power that succours and understands, penetrating through all the disguises of wilfulness and opposition. It is life itself, the vigilant wakefulness. Listen! There are my last words, the end of a life of poetry through which I looked —and found!' He paused again, to recall the verses that he wanted to repeat to me. The wind blew a smother of soft-fingered flakes at the window pane, as an accompaniment.

'Then life is—to wake not sleep,
Rise and not rest, but press
From earth's level where blindly creep
Things perfected, more or less,
To the heaven's height, far and steep,

Where, amid what strifes and storms
May wait the adventurous quest,
Power is Love—transports, transforms
Who aspired from worst to best,
Sought the soul's world, spurned the worms'.

I have faith such end shall be:
From the first, Power was—I knew.
Life has made clear to me
That, strive but for closer view,
Love were as plain to see.'

With that, I was alone, the echo of the word Love ringing in my mind, as the last attachment of an illusion which had drawn me across snow-quilted Venice on this December day.

I AM AN incorrigible riparian. My only excuse for not
living on a river-bank is that I have to get on with some work,
and that I must not have too much distraction from that purpose. While in Chambers in London, in the Inns of Court, I
found myself every day wandering down to the Thames
Embankment, making the excuse that my dog needed air and
exercise. So he did, and fully he enjoyed them; but the excuse
was not quite so altruistic as it sounded. It was that of an
addict of flowing waters, one who craves to watch the tides,
or the flow of an urgent stream, any waters that are moving
under the direction of the invisible forces that spin the worlds
and keep the skies in place.

And this occupation, of just standing and staring at the
waters, is one in which I can spend not minutes but hours, to
the detriment of my reputation and the neglect of my profes-
sion. So I have to live on a hill, above the reach of temptation.
But whenever I go on holiday, I find myself, unconsciously,
gravitating towards rivers, or inland lakes, or some aspect of a
seashore where the ocean and land make some vehement duo-
logue together, offering a dramatic conflict even when at rest.

So it was while on holiday recently. After leaving the lakes
of northern Italy and the canals of Venice, I stayed in Paris for
a few days during my return journey. Paris is the queen of
cities, and the Seine with the diadem of bridges is the crown
worn by that queen. It is a shapely, artificed crown, made by
craftsmen through the ages, with a skill that has given it not
only the splendour of royal France, but also the homeliness of
provincial France, busy with domestic life and communal
habits.

I never weary of watching that. Year after year I go across

the Channel to spend sometimes only a day or two on that hobby of mine; just watching the river flow by, with its little dramas of flotsam and jetsam, its tricks of light and temperature, its lispings of half-hidden music, all set amid the roar of Paris traffic and the eternal feminine perfume of her streets. I want now, however, to stop not for this pleasure, but for one more intimate, more elusive of description.

I came back from the bookstalls of the Quai Voltaire one morning to find an invitation from a Russian novelist, who had been in France since the Communist Revolution made his life at home impossible. I was asked out to luncheon at his house near Malmaison, and I went, for I had long admired his books, which are translated into English. It took me some time to find the corner of the suburban quarter just beyond Josephine's palace, but I was not unduly late in discovering a narrow lane between widely spaced villas on the right hand, and a garden hedge on the left. The place I sought was in that garden, as I saw from the name-plate on the wall of the wide gates beside a porter's lodge. A man came out from the lodge, and he wore a green baize apron. He had wide cheek-bones and massive shoulders. He was a Russian peasant, the first of the native servants whom I encountered during my visit to a household which might have been taken complete from the pages of *The House of Gentlefolk,* by Turgeniev, or from those rich, biographical chapters in the country-life books of the nineteenth-century writer Aksakov, wherein are set for ever the scenes of Russian country households during the days of the last of the Tsars.

I entered the house, and there came to meet me a frail, elderly figure dressed in black velvet coat and waistcoat, salt and pepper trousers, exquisitely cut; pince-nez that at once reminded me of photographs of Chekov. The old gentleman groped for my hand. He was nearly blind with cataracts, a drawback for which he apologized as he led me through the house to a huge library at the back.

At first my attention was taken by the books that filled the walls from floor to ceiling. Then I noticed a large round table filled with periodicals in many languages. Most of the English weeklies lay there, and for a moment I had a sort of busman's holiday feeling as I saw my own bread-and-butter contributions amongst them.

But my host was talking gently, somewhat wearily, in the manner of a man of the world who has grown out of the world and is turning inward, making greater preparations. He raised his arm towards the high windows, whose glazed doors opened upon lawns, two gigantic cedar trees, a row of white poplars, and beyond them, down below a narrow bank of grass paved with daffodils, the river!

The river, the Seine, on its way to Paris, but still provincial, still whispering of farms, and fishermen, and cattle being driven down at dusk of dawn, and platoons of geese coming under their own command to drink and protest with Rome-rousing voices! The water flowed steadily, at just the pace which it keeps through the embankments round the two sacred islands of St. Louis and The City, past Notre Dame and the Tuileries. But here, seen from the dark library, through the windows heavy with white jasmine, and past the melancholy lawns of a French country garden (for the lawns of France are never cut close, with the result that they are a deeper green than our English ones) here, the Seine was a dryad stream, its waters glaucous with reflections from a further row of still larger poplars on the opposite bank. I saw, amid the interweavings of shade and light made by the moving water, darker masses that momentarily indented and swelled. They were the reflections of clots of mistletoe: a marvellous sight, like the knots in old lace.

Then, still to the accompaniment of the courteous old voice, and a glass of sherry which my host had asked me to pour out, I saw through my half-attentive eye a boat drifting down, and on it, dangerously balanced, a chest of drawers.

The man at the back held the cargo with one hand, while he oared with the other in a sweep held in a rowlock at the stern of the boat. On top of the piece of furniture lay a huge nosegay of daffodils. Was he going to a wedding, I wondered, and taking his present with him? But the river had carried them away before I could answer, and the next offering was a painted canal barge, with a pair of lovers sitting side by side at the helm, arms intertwined, and the punctuations of the journey marked by a kiss from time to time. I counted three along my line of vision.

Now, however, I had to give the whole of my attention to the necessary courtesies, for my hostess appeared to complete the harmony of this astonishing menage; astonishing because it was snatched back from a vanished world, and set here by the banks of an immortal river of timeless waters, with beauty, utility, nature and man floating by for ever, a clock of the centuries. I shook her hand, looked at her sweet, welcoming face, so fitting a counterpiece to the ravaged features of her husband. I knew I was in the presence of a perfect relationship, and that nothing would be taken amiss if, as was inevitable, my attention should wander during the coming meal, and my eye should take on that distant look of one listening to music, the music of rivers.

A CUPFUL OF LEAVES

Coming back, early in November, after a month in London, I walked round the paved terrace early next morning, keeping to the flagstones in order not to wet my slippers. The sun had just risen and was shining, or rather gold-fuming through the trees of the cherry orchard, and throwing long bars of shadow right across the lower lawn, from the Irish yews.

I had returned to a different world. I left it in mid-October with the housewalls hung with purple grapes, and the roses still in full explosion amongst a setting of rejuvenated annuals flowering afresh after the rains following the long drought. Hardly a sign of decay was then to be seen. An occasional lemon-tinted leaf floated down from the weeping willow, to curl like a gondola on the surface of the pond; but that had been happening all through the summer, and I took it as no sign of the fall of the year. No, they reminded me rather of a passage of verse from our beloved English contemporary poet, Edith Sitwell, to whom one can go again and again for a rich comment on one's own experience:

179

'Dark are their plumes, and dark the airs that grew
Amid those weeping leaves.
Plantations of the East drop precious dew
That ripened by the light, rich leaves perspire,
Such are the drops that from the bright swans' feathers
flew.'

And a swan's feather does not make an autumn! No,
summer had lingered on after its already magnificent achievements through an abnormal year, and I had begun to think
that perhaps time was standing still, the result, as our rustic
roadman told me, 'of them there Atom chaps' and their
experiments in various parts of the world.

This illusion vanished as soon as I went out of doors a
month later, with my five senses doubly stimulated by the
change of season, and the freshness of the familiar scene
which had been deserted for four weeks.

The silence took me by the heart. It was like a caress, after
the buffetings of town. I had thought that my room in a quiet
Mayfair side street was peaceful enough, and indeed I had
slept there soundly enough after days of professional activity
that sometimes sent me to bed exhausted. But this morning,
the first at home, came round me with a real, positive silence so
absolute that I could fancy I heard the dew preparing to rise
from the grass, and the sun snapping the threads of cloud
which still tethered it to the horizon. A distant cock crowed,
with a moist, chill cry, and awoke responses from farms and
cottages along the valley. A robin flickered down from the
holly tree and looked beadily at the cup of tea in my hand.
I set the cup, after emptying it, down on the ground below
the great old pear tree that overhangs the end of the terrace.
The robin hopped up on the rim, stared into the cup, his
head on one side, inquiringly, and signified his disappointment with a little, incredulous whistle, as though doubting if
human nature could be so indifferent to his demands. Then

he flew back into the holly, and I looked up to see his rusty waistcoat gleaming among the wet, enamelled foliage. Not until that moment did I notice how once again, the holly tree had emerged as the most luxuriant object in the landscape. Below it, the hedges were thinning, held together by a few bedraggled strings of briony and honeysuckle, whose berries were swollen with rain, and discoloured by the first frosts. The crab-apple tree and the quince, farther down the hedge, were already Lear-like in their locks, 'with yellow leaves, or none, or few'.

I forgot the injunction not to get my slippers wet, and I ventured across the lawn to look over the curving yew hedge at the vegetable garden that lay below and opened on to the cornfield, and the long valley. A wind rose suddenly, coming after the sun. Silence shrank away, and a rustling, dry and papery, sprang up around me, sifting through the hedges, the dry clusters of the scarlet runners, the thinning boughs of every fruit tree. The air freshened further, sighing and lifting. It took a flight of blackened leaves, like starlings in miniature, out of a pippin tree. I looked back up the garden, and saw a still larger flight blow out from the pear by the terrace; blow out, scatter, and tumble heavily to earth as though too weary of time to be able to seek a further sleeping place for winter and the metamorphosis which was their destiny.

I shivered. The wind had a hint of warning in it. There was a moan in its throat, an ominous touch that set me looking again at the landscape. Why had I not instantly seen the change, when I opened the door ten minutes earlier? Had I been still bespectacled by memory of a month ago? Was I still gazing, as by a time-lag of vision, at the lush fruits, the grapes, figs, comice pears, and over-perfect roses of late September; all now vanished, but leaving a ghost perfume and bloom of colour behind them?

The oddity of this, with its emphasis upon the uncertainty of human sense-impressions, turned my attention inwards for a few moments, and I stood there, in wet slippers, meditating upon this puzzle, while the sullen drama of a November dawn continued to unfold its furtive plot around me. When I returned to the present scene, it had already altered, carrying the process of decay a stage further. The wind had not ceased; indeed, it was gathering itself up in a more earnest and concentrated way, attacking the earth with rough vigour. I could see all along the ridge of the upper woods a cloud, or rather a dark smudge, spiralling up feebly, and dropping again. It was another apron of foliage, torn off and flung aside. The distant trees seemed appreciably darker after that bout, darker and more denuded.

I shook my damp feet, for it was useless to shake my head. Carefully I retraced my footsteps across the wet lawn, thinking thereby to escape some of the moisture. I could feel the chill creeping up my legs, and I touched my hair with a blue hand to make sure that some of that foliage was not being snatched away too. On my way in, I stooped and picked up the cup and saucer from beneath the pear tree. They were filled with fallen leaves.

FINIS